GW00319743

Ghosts of Hampshire and the Isle of Wight

Web of Fear

Ghosts of Hampshire and the Isle of Wight

Web of Fear

Donald A.Parr

The Breedon Books
Publishing Company
Derby

First published in Great Britain by
The Breedon Books Publishing Company Limited
Breedon House, 44 Friar Gate, Derby, DE1 1DA.
1996

Thanks to
Jean & Lisa
Angela & Peter
who saw me
through 1992.

I have been here before,
But when or how I cannot tell,
I know the grass beyond the door,
The sweet keen smell,
The sighing sound,
the lights around, the shore.

Dante Gabriel Rossetti
1828-1882

ISBN 1 85983 068 4

Printed and bound by Butler & Tanner Ltd., Selwood Printing
Works, Caxton Road, Frome, Somerset.

Colour separations by Colour Services, Wigston, Leicester.

Jackets printed by Lawrence-Allen,Weston-super-Mare, Avon.

Contents

Foreword

As chairman of the well-known Solent Male Voice Choir and Grand Knight local region of the Knights of Saint Columba, it has been and still is my great privilege to meet numerous people from differing backgrounds, nearly all of whom indulge in hobbies or pastimes which are as diverse as they are themselves.

It is possible, however, during conversation, to discover a vast amount of common ground. Likes and dislikes which are applicable to most of us. Probably high on the list are our children, our families and friends and – a subject which never ceases to amaze me, Ghosts!

Whatever ghosts are, whether they are feared and hated, liked or simply dismissed as imagination, the subject is always guaranteed to provide a talking point for many a rainy day. There are few, even among older children who have not heard of the ghost of Hamlet's father in Shakespeare's tragedy, or those spirits in *A Christmas Carol* by Dickens whose visits serve a good purpose. Ebeneezer Scrooge was visited by four of them, all in one night. A ghost story on radio or television is sure to command an audience and I have merely cited examples of some well loved literary fictitious spectres.

What of those ghosts which are not so fictitious – at least in the minds of some of those people contributing to this book by Don Parr?

Even as a practising Christian, I admit to being as fascinated as everyone else when it comes to the supernatural or paranormal which is why, when Don – whom I have known as a good friend for quite a number of years – asked me to join his research team, I jumped at the chance. I will admit to never having seen a ghost myself, but experiencing some of the old buildings and weird places where many sane people have reported seeing them, I will never decry the possibility of their existence, after all, I have now met many professional folk and family men and women with their feet planted firmly on the ground who will swear to having had experiences with disembodied beings. They do not strike me as being the victims of a 'fertile imagination' so why should they try to carry us along with make-believe, and why have so many different people at different times sworn to having experienced the same phenomena?

Maybe there is no rational answer. In this excellent book, Don does not offer explanation but simply gives the facts as reported to him, either personally or through history, puts them down in an easily readable fashion, poses a few questions and leaves you to try to answer. Is it possible that maybe you can?

Colin Newman
Havant, Hampshire
June 1966.

Introduction

WHERE does one begin to recount stories which have neither beginning or end but just misty details on which to form a basis to relate the uncertainties that are present for us to see? Or are they? Are they meant to remain solely in the realms of the mind, appearing to us mortals only at times of stress or darkness?

Let us try to merge into this web of fear which surrounds the very nature of these bizarre happenings. Let us see if we can untangle that web which shrouds the mind, bringing with it the dread of that which defies explanation.

Throughout the centuries man has lived and worked the land for his allotted span of life, and then died. He has known the land by many different names. On the Isle of Wight, villages spread as the population expanded and small towns developed. On the Island there is always an atmosphere, but one which can change quickly, from the innocent domesticity of the countryside to the forlorn desolation of the sea pounding upon the foreshore.

During daylight hours a sense of freedom prevails across the pleasant fields. A place to live out one's life in a garden paradise. But – man is man. He can be the most evil and devious being on earth. Precisely what lies beyond our allotted span we do not know, but some who have been dispatched there by others who plotted against them, though they have departed this life, appear not to have left it. Or have they?

When I first came into contact with the supernatural I admit that I was one of the most cynical disbelievers, even in the possibility of the existence of such phenomena. It was not until I personally came across happenings which could not be explained that I began to take an active interest in the subject.

Whilst trying to keep my feet firmly on the ground, I have spent much time sifting through vast quantities of reports of sightings of ghosts and hauntings, some of which have turned out to be the fermented imagination of those wishing to experience events which exist only in their minds. Others are happenings which have no place in this present day standard world of automation. It is a sobering thought that ghost stories, which for the most part cannot be explained, are part of our heritage. No science can unravel them, neither can any categorisation take place.

What is a ghost? This is a question which I am unable to answer. Having spent much time travelling and interviewing people who state that they have seen apparitions, and having read many reports of such sightings, I am still no nearer to being able to answer the question, What is a ghost? Some describe them as 'misty apparitions', as if an actual mist was lifting from a small pond on an autumn evening; others say they are solid objects capable of physical force and able to move things; at other times they have been described simply as peaceful figures looking neither left nor right. But whatever form they take, no one who has made a study of the supernatural can ever deny their existence. To my mind there is no shadow of doubt that there are planes or spheres, where disembodied entities exist outside the physical world with which we are so familiar. Spirits, invariably of low intelligence, do materialise, and there have been far too many well documented and authenticated instances for them all to be dismissed as fantasies. Does there exist an eternal element within us all? If this is the case, then what happens at death to this element, or spirit if you prefer to call it that? The Christian religion teaches us that the spirit goes to Heaven to be judged on its lifestyle led on earth and on such judgement either to eternal rest or everlasting suffering. But there are those who say "That's all very well, but how about those who have had no life on earth; such as young children? What about those who have never heard of Christianity and others who have led a blameless life until, in one moment of madness or desperation they commit an unforgivable sin?"

Other religions teach that the spirit is like an eternal spark which has inhabited many bodies, and as the body is only a temporary lodging, when it no longer exists, the spark is reincarnated into another body which provides the vehicle for it to progress towards perfection. When sufficient progress has been achieved then perfect peace is attained. Many believe in this latter hypothesis as the only explanation for life on earth and life after death, but I am not convinced. However, it would be nice to think of caring spirits continuing to influence those of us still in the land of the living.

Donald A.Parr
Totland Bay
April 1996

Acknowledgements

I would would like to thank the following people who have given up their valuable time in assisting me to compile the *Web of Fear*, not only for relating their experiences but for showing me such warm hospitality: Ivor and Jill Allison (re Golden Hill Fort); Mike Burr of the Red Lion, Brading; Doug and Sheila Cook of the Eclipse Inn, Winchester; Dave Death; Valerie Dove of the Hyde Tavern, Winchester; David Grant; Huber Hughes of the Royal Anchor, Liphook; Sheila Hughes; Patrick Kirkby, historian of Netley Hospital; Mr and Mrs Paine; Millie Pugsley and Roy Dore (re Ventnor Hospital); the landlord and landlady of the Red Lion, Horndean; Ray Linnington, owner of St Lawrence Dene; Lord Montagu and Sue Tompkin of Beaulieu House; Kate Mortimer, bar manageress of the Crown Hotel, Alton; the late Count Slade de Pomeroy; Jeanne Schroeder of Arreton Manor; Graham Osborn-Smith; Wax Museum, Brading; Kenneth Battle and Patrick McNulty of the Priory Hotel, Nettlestone; Jennifer and Michael Lister; Lord Louis Library, Newport; Capt Peter Starling, curator of the RAMC Museum, Keogh Barracks, Ash Vale; Southampton University; Ventnor Botanical Gardens; my friend in Yarmouth who wishes to be known only as 'Peter'; Colin Newman of Leigh Park, Havant, for supplying transport and assisting me in a considerable amount of research during my many wanderings along the by-ways of Hampshire and also for writing the Foreword; and Ken Robson for his help with the cartography; also the Portsmouth Dockyard Security Police.

I would like also to thank the authors and publishers of the following books, some of whom I have quoted and most I have used as works of reference: *A Brief Life* by Graham Bebbington; *Ghosts of Hampshire and The Isle of Wight* by Peter Underwood; *Ghosts of The Isle of Wight* by Gay Steadman and Ray Anker; *Phantoms of the High Seas* by Phillip MacDougal; *Manor Houses of the Isle of Wight* by Roy Winter; *Wanderings in the Isle of Wight* by the late Ethel C.Hargrove and Clive Barton, late of the *Isle of Wight County Press*; *The Haunted South* by John Forman; also to Neil Hammerton of Hammerton Book Services, Newport, for allowing extracts from *The Darker Side of Wight*; several photographs have been supplied by Mike Hope (whose *Villages of Hampshire* is also published by Breedon).

Finally my thanks must go to my agent, Peter T.G.White MA, without whose help and encouragement this book would never have been finished.

Witness to Murder

THOSE who stroll along the by-ways of Arreton, enjoying the surrounding countryside, will be no strangers to the atmosphere of peace and happiness. So it has been for the past 1,200 years of recorded history. Arreton Valley is the setting for one of England's finest examples of manor houses. We know that Arreton Manor was acquired by Edward the Confessor in 1050, but there are indications of a manor long before this. At one time it was owned by the church and, under the auspices of an abbot, housed a community of brothers and monks. Although now slumbering peacefully, through the mists of time, many dark deeds have been perpetrated within its walls.

In a charming room located off the great hall there sometimes appears a silvery grey figure, possibly that of a monk believed to be one of the former occupants of the manor when it was owned by the church. This apparition is

Arreton Manor House.

accompanied by the sweet smell of incense and the sound of chanting. Who this spirit is or why it should find no rest, we have no knowledge.

It is recorded that Count Slade de Pomeroy, one of the former owners of Arreton Manor, would often be awakened by the sound of tapping on his bedroom door.

"I would just lay there ignoring it," he said. "I knew without doubt that should I open the door there would be – nothing! Just an empty passage."

Once, however, when he did open the door he was pushed fiercely back by unseen hands. His housekeeper, who was present at the time, told him not to worry as she had just seen two monks enter the room, one of whom had pushed him from the doorway.

Some years later a visitor, who, having no previous knowledge of any manifestations at the manor, came to a landing from which, leading off to the left, was a small room with a larger one opposite. Suddenly she began to feel distinctly uncomfortable, and on entering the small room, her complexion turned pallid and she became so disorientated that she was unable to stay. A sense of fear overwhelmed her. Quickly she crossed the landing and into the larger room. When asked if she was alright she replied that the feeling was still there but not as strong. She likened her fear to that of being constantly watched.

It was later that the count related this story which he had learned. On the landing between the two rooms, James and Thomas, the two elder brothers of a Mr Barnaby Leigh, fought a duel over who should inherit the property. The fight ended with a sword being thrust through the heart of one brother; the other died three days later from wounds received in the duel.

We know for certain that in Elizabethan times the title to Arreton Manor lay with Barnaby Leigh, a wealthy man. It is said that one day, when old Barnaby lay ill in his bed, not yet ready to 'meet his maker', his son, John, could restrain himself no longer and smothered the old man with a pillow in order to inherit his father's wealth. To his horror, when looking up after his deed, he saw his young sister, Annabel, standing there and in his panic dragged her upstairs to the top of the house and threw her from the highest window to her death. So it is said that there is an area of coldness in that room which no heat can remove. The ghost of little Annabel is often seen and heard as she roams the grounds of Arreton Manor. Her apparition is that of a small figure in a blue dress and white slippers laced with ribbons. She has been glimpsed walking briefly through different parts of the house, sometimes in the garden and usually accompanied by the plaintif cry of "Mamma, Mamma". Other times she is simply manifested as a peaceful ghost returning to the lovely house she once knew.

The manor house is open periodically to visitors and on occasions strangers

Window at Arreton Manor overlooking the courtyard. The Room now houses the Doll Museum.

ask about the sweet little girl in the blue dress who seems to vanish inexplicably. Once, a child ran to her mother saying she had seen a little girl in a blue dress. She approached her to try to make friends, but the girl in blue disappeared into a brick wall. On another occasion there was a report that one evening a woman, working at the manor and thinking of nothing in particular, heard footsteps and a cry of "Mamma, Mamma," but she subsequently ascertained that at the time all the children in the house were in bed and asleep. On another occasion, when hearing a sound one autumn evening, she looked up and saw the figure of Annabel standing at the top of the main staircase. The light was on and she had no hesitation in describing details of what she saw. From previous descriptions, it was the figure of Annabel, wearing her blue dress, with her sweet little innocent face and long fair hair falling in tight curls over her shoulder.

There is little doubt that the tragedy and violence perpetrated within the walls of Arreton Manor seem to have left their mark. Those who were so cruelly put to death seem unable to find peace and must return to haunt this beautiful house.

No Rest for Louis

A S we move from the heart of this lovely Island we can be forgiven for failing to notice the invisible threads of fear, which not only link town to town and generation to generation, but present times to the age of the Phoenicians, 4,000 years ago. Brading, on the eastern shore, is today a small, picturesque town, the once-busy quayside now silted up to a stage where buildings can be supported. The village boasts a church nearly 800 years old and also a house the foundations of which pre-date jit by many centuries. Antiquarians will say that the narrow road leading past the vicarage was once used by the Phoenicians who traded here. Relics of times past are everywhere, including 12 burial mounds of Bronze Age Britain, and a third-century Roman villa discovered in 1880.

At one end of the High Street stands

The Isle of Wight Wax Museum at Brading. In the background is St Mary's Parish Church.

The old Crown Inn, now part of the courtyard of the Wax Museum at Brading.

Brading Town Hall with its gruesome display of the town's original public whipping post and stocks, whilst opposite is the Isle of Wight Wax Museum housed in a building the origins of which date back to 1499. Prior to this an older building stood on the site. As a dwelling it is steeped in history and intrigue and over many decades has known numerous uses as diverse as a bawdy inn, a guild house and a brew house.

Long ago when Brading Marsh was a sizable seaport, the house was known as the Crown Inn and the rooms would be full of gamblers, prostitutes, thieves and every kind of riff-raff who frequented the seaports of the world. There is a story that, to this inn at Brading there came a Frenchman, one Louis de Rochefort, a gentleman. No one knows why he went to Brading, although it is thought that he could possibly have been an emissary of the King of France, delivering a message to Charles I imprisoned in Carisbrooke Castle.

It seemed that he had dined well and was shown to an upstairs room overlooking Quay Lane, the same lane used by those Phoenician traders of long ago. He undressed and after his weary journey, was soon asleep. A little later a shadowy figure crept into the gentleman's room, an open knife in his hand.

Suddenly, the figure sprang from the shadows towards the sleeping Frenchman. The blade glinted in the moonlight as it plunged down again and again. De Rochefort's dying screams echoed throughout the inn as the assassin fled.

Was this murderer hired by Cromwell as has been suggested? No one knows.

The felon closed the heavy door with blood-stained hands; the victim sank back in agony on to his bed, the

The resting place of the bones of Louis La Roche, in the courtyard of the Wax Museum at Brading.

knife still protruding from his chest. All is vividly recalled in a Wax Museum tableau, but in reality the Frenchman, with his dying breath cursed the murderer and swore to haunt the building until his mortal remains were returned to his beloved homeland to be interred in his native French soil.

Throughout the centuries Louis de Rochfort has kept this promise, haunting not only the old inn but all subsequent buildings constructed thereon, walking their creaking boards seeking vengeance.

Generation upon generation have lived on the site of the Crown Inn, but still the haunting continues. For over 100 years the house was owned by a family named Carley who recorded numerous

manifestations of an aristocratic figure in one of the bedrooms overlooking Quay Lane.

On the still air of a quiet night, it is said, one can often hear his screams and the sound of an invisible coach rattling along the lane outside the house as the assassin fled from the scene of the evil deed.

Tenants have been known to move in a hurry, unable to live with the appearances of Louis de Rochefort. Even animals seem afraid to approach the first floor, as if knowing something we do not. In the past many people have requested permission to stay overnight in the museum and of those who have tried, most have fled before the first rays of dawn streaked over the eastern sky. In fact, the editor of a local newspaper, together with a friend and his dog, were given special permission to stay one night. When telling me this, Graham Osborn-Smith, the museum curator, laughingly related the fact that the editor bid a hasty retreat a little after midnight and his friend who felt a little safer with his dog was hard on his heels about an hour later. "They heard noises, rattles and experienced the stone-cold atmosphere. The dog became hard to control and they thought that we were playing pranks on them," he said. "Personally, I have never seen the ghost but this house is old and to say the least 'spooky' at night. At times when I have been locking up I have definitely experienced something. I have often wondered who runs faster, the ghost or me!" Workmen installing a new water main 30 years ago, uncovered a human skeleton. Was it the remains of Louis de Rochefort?

Graham said that he recognised the bones as human, as he was once a medical student. He contacted his doctor brother who confirmed his impression. After notifying the police, Graham was most surprised when they took no action, advising that as the remains were so old he had best contact the coroner. He continued "After getting in touch with the coroner and my solicitor, Mr Percy Rolf of Robertson, Jarvis and Rolf, it was decided that these were the mortal remains of de Rochefort and that they should be returned if possible to his native France for a Christian burial. This soon saw my wife and myself at the airport in Paris endeavouring to explain the bones in the specially-made box to airport customs officers. I managed to make contact with the editor of *Le Figaro*, a French daily newspaper, who followed up the story in article form. Many Rocheforts came forward but none seemed to want to claim the mortal remains of their ancestor."

The bones were therefore brought back to Brading by Graham who experienced even worse comments from the British Customs. For a while, much to the consternation of his wife, he stored them under their bed. In reply to my rather obvious question as to why he did not arrange to reinter them, he replied: "Ah, but I did. After much official discussion and soul searching de Rochefort's remains were reinterred in the original grave but now laying on imported French soil. I hope he now rests in peace."

In 1991 a visitor from Australia came to the museum and demanded to see 'the boss'. Graham, as ever available to his visitors, saw him.

"The man in question introduced himself as 'Louis de Rochefort'. I believe he said 'Louis', but I cannot be too sure. He had been searching for this ancestor for years and it was not until he was staying at an hotel in Portsmouth that he read one of our pamphlets. He rushed over immediately and after many conversations thought the remains must be those of his kinsman of so many years ago. He promised to come again in a few years with his wife and family."

Maybe now that Louis de Rochefort is claimed, wanted and loved again, he will rest assured in the premise that in a Brading courtyard his grave is covered by a glass-topped coffin through which visitors are able to look down at his remains. Thanks to Graham Osborn-Smith, these are preserved more as a shrine to his memory, than merely one more museum exhibit.

Another Time – Another Place?

TRAVELLING inland for just a few miles, we cross the beautiful Ashey Down, and arrive at the spot where a doctor and his wife experienced spectral phenomena so unique, that the incident bears no logical explanation.

One January evening in 1969, Dr and Mrs White left their home at St Helen's to have dinner with some friends. It was the night of the full moon and although the weather was cold and crisp, visibility was good. As they reached the top of Ashey Down they found themselves entwined in a mystery, so bizarre that the memory of it was to remain with them for the rest of their lives. Mrs White first saw the lights which materialised in the middle of a lonely stretch of the downs. The nearest farm house was some miles away, yet all about them in the fields were numerous flickering lights.

Her husband told her that it was probably just a farmer and his workers looking for a sheep which had strayed or something else just as easily explainable, so, for the moment it was left at that.

They negotiated the narrow winding road leading to Mersley Down. About halfway down a long hill they were startled to see similar lights in the fields on their right. It was as if the whole area was ablaze and a town had suddenly been built. Stopping the car they sat, mesmerised looking at the thousands of illuminations. They remembered there was a lane leading off to the right, but which now had assumed all the proportions of a proper road with street lighting. It seemed to lead to a large built-up area, illuminated with red, green, orange and white lights. Something was happening, the sight that lay before them was just as if it were part of a vast film set – or some Technicolour dream. By now the sky was turning black as clouds scurried across the moon.

The doctor decided to take a closer look to discover the reason for this phenomenon. Starting the car he proceeded down the hill and turned into the illuminated road which he knew did not exist. Could this be the cart track that he remembered? As he stopped the car and they both alighted, the lights disappeared just as suddenly as they had appeared. There they both were, standing on a cart track!

They were bewildered to say the least, so taking each other's hand decided to explore further but found no sign of anything other than the green fields, now serene as the clouds cleared.

The country lane on Mersley Down where Dr and Mrs White witnessed the strange lights.

Anxious to spot a familiar landmark they returned to the car and made their way over the downs towards the Hare and Hounds, the little thatched inn at the crossroads on the way to Newport.

Suddenly the vision returned. The fields on the right were again filled with lights. The doctor and his wife could see the Hare and Hounds in the distance but it was nothing like the inn they knew and loved. Instead it seemed to be bathed in a strange light. People were running back and forth across the road carrying torches.

Steeling himself, the doctor slowed the car and was again about to stop, and find out what was happening when a very tall man, wearing a long jerkin with a leather belt ran straight towards him. As if not seeing them he ran, quite literally through the front of the car! The doctor braked sharply but there was no sensation of any impact. He drove slowly forward again towards the Hare and Hounds and was about to enter the car park of the inn when, just as suddenly, the spectre again vanished, as if some-one had thrown a switch. Shaking with fear the doctor and his wife got out of their car and hurriedly made their way into the Hare and Hounds. Once inside everything was normal, solid, friendly – the only illuminations were those always there. Through the window of the lighted inn they could see out over the fields into just a black void – not a light to be seen.

After a suitable time in which to compose themselves they continued their journey which was to take them to the southern end of the Island and the village of Niton where they related their tale to their friends.

No satisfactory explanation was forthcoming, nor has any been found to this day. Some suggest it was a mirage, maybe the lights of Portsmouth reflecting across the water of the Solent. If so, how about the man in the long jerkin and leather belt who ran through the doctor's moving car? Here we have a doctor of medicine, a good doctor and respected as a leading citizen with a sober outlook on life, not given to flights of fancy. Also his wife, by no means herself lacking in erudition. Had they both glimpsed something from another time, or even maybe from another dimension. No one has ever found out, but whatever caused the spectre was to shake the good doctor far more than he would ever admit. It was something he just could not understand – could not even begin to explain. Had they both somehow entered a timewarp, and broken through the web of fear?

Horrors of Knighton Gorges

LEAVING Mersley Down and returning towards Ashey Down and Brading, we come to a turning on the right known as Knighton Chute which leads eventually to the village of Newchurch.

Newchurch is reputed to be one of the most haunted spots on the Island, for we now enter the realm of Knighton Gorges, and the many apparitions frequenting the dark lanes on winter nights. It is here we come across a legend that a wizard once cursed a knight in order that he would never sleep in eternity and was doomed to be mounted on a black horse, to gallop down those same lanes, night after night. He is still to be seen after all these hundreds of years. In recent times sightings seem to be less frequent, however, there are still many local people alive today who will swear to have witnessed the black knight galloping towards the manor.

Whether they be young or old men, women or children who wander abroad on a moonlit night some have reported the frightening apparition and have heard the hooves becoming louder as the phantom passes by. Some say the rider is headless – others not, but those who see can only stand wide eyed. Most of the local villagers would prefer to remain in their houses than to glimpse the black knight.

Hugh de Morville, one of the murderers of Sir Thomas à Becket, owned a manor at Knighton, in its day one of the finest to be found in the south of England. After being commissioned by Henry II to commit this dastardly deed and then being denounced by him, de Morville fled to the safe haven of Carisbrooke Castle until the uproar following the murder subsided. He then returned to his home at Knighton where he lived for the next 30 years, never to be brought to justice for his deeds. Has this evil influence lived on through the centuries, for when his son, John, died in 1200, the male line finished.

This manor house has a long and chequered history. The sturdy walls, exuded an air of oppression and evil, were steeped in tales of the cruelty and terror that went on within. At the time of the Crusades, one Sir Ralph de Gorges was to become the owner of the manor, the name of which he changed to Knighton Gorges. It is believed that Sir Ralph died at the hands of the Saracens, but the house was to remain in the De Gorges family for over 100 years. Since that time the name Knighton Gorges has been synonymous with mystery, death, ghosts and shocking apparitions.

It was while the house was owned by the De Gorges that one member of the staff who believed that he had trapped a ghost in a top room, placed a Latin inscription over the door ensuring that the apparition would be imprisoned there for all time.

Some years later, Sir Theobold Russell, Lord of Yelverland, married into the De Gorges family and took the name of Gorges, becoming known as Sir Theobold de Gorges. It is recorded that Theobold was Lord of Knighton in 1365, and from that day onwards it seemed that his fate was sealed. He was chosen to organise the defences of the district surrounding Quarr Abbey with Reynold Oglander, Lord of Nunwell, as his lieutenant. Soon after his marriage the town of St Helen's was attacked by the French. After the battle had been won, they found Sir Theobold mortally wounded and carried him back to the manor, bleeding so badly that he left a trail of blood upon the stairs. In spite of many attempts at removal, these blood-stains were to stay until the manor was demolished in the 19th century.

Sir Theobold had defeated the French but not without heavy casualties on both sides. It was his wish that he be taken to his room, where he died. From then on the room became known as 'the room of tears'. From that day occupants of the manor would often hear coming from within the 'room of tears' the sound of sobbing, so heart rending that

all hearing it could not help but join in and cry with the phantom. As soon as they started, the phantom would cease.

As the centuries passed, more families, such as the Hackets and the Gilberts were to become owners of the property and during these times there were many strange stories associated with the house.

In 1563 ownership of the manor passed to the Dillingtons of Dorset. Little is known about the Dillington dynasty until 1712 when the master of Knighton Gorges was one Sir Tristram Dillington, MP for Newport.

Tristram was a good master, generous to a fault and popular with rich and poor alike. That was until 1721 when a fever epidemic struck the Island – a fever so rife that within a fortnight his wife and their four children including his heir, were struck down and all died. They lie buried in the local churchyard.

Sir Tristram was never to recover from this tragedy, for within weeks he had changed from the dashing figure of a merry Guards major to a bitter and melancholy man, one who would never exchange so much as a word with anyone. So low fell his spirits, so great was his despair that on 4 July he drowned himself. His butler, knowing that his master's grief was so great watched over him, but Sir Tristram's plunge into the manorial lake was too swift. Entering the water after him, the butler somehow pulled him to the shore – but it was too late. His master was dead. Knowing how the law stood (in those days in cases of suicide all possessions were confiscated by the Crown,) the butler, whether thinking of his own position or of Sir Tristram's two unmarried sisters, Mary and Hannah, decided to cover up the deed. Summoning the head gardener they concocted a plan which would save the family fortune. Quickly saddling Sir Tristram's favourite horse and then breaking its girth, they set it loose beside the lake, then raised the alarm, informing everyone that there had been an accident and that the master had drowned.

There is a variation to this story. Some say that Sir Tristram shot himself and the butler made it look like an accident, but whatever story is true the butler's word was accepted and the estate was saved. In due course he was rewarded with a farm of his own.

Rest however, was not to be granted to Sir Tristram. Soon many of the tenants on the estate reported seeing him with a troubled face and a weary tread moving around the grounds of the manor where once he had been so happy.

With the ghost of Sir Tristram, the headless horseman, the mournful wails coming from the room of tears, the cries of anguish which still come from the sealed room and linger in the night air when least expected the hauntings continue.

By the middle of the 18th century Knighton Gorges had passed via the female line to General Maurice Bockland who used this great house to entertain famous people of the day including Sir Joshua Reynolds, actor David Garrick and John Wilkes MP, but this happiness was not to last for long. Bockland's daughter married into an old Scottish family and in due course the house passed to their son, Maurice George Bissett, and the final phase of this mournful manor house had begun.

It is reported that Bissett was an unscrupulous, selfish bigot. He became the butt of London society when he caused a scandal by running off with the beautiful wife of Sir Richard Wolsley. This sensational case did no good to anyone except the hawkers of the streets of London who openly sold copies of the evidence and with it a savage caricature. In the end the jury found for Sir Richard, but instead of the £20,000 he had demanded he was awarded one shilling. Bissett's troubles were not over. He disapproved of his daughter's choice of husband, a clergyman named Fenwick and, more to the point, her cousin. He forbade them to marry but despite his insistence, the couple eloped and were married anyway. So fierce was Bissett's wrath that he disinherited her and swore on oath that neither she, her husband nor any children from their marriage would ever again set foot in Knighton Gorges.

The couple decided that they would wait until the death of the old man. However, Bissett, on learning in 1821 that he had a terminal illness enlisted a private army of workmen and completely demolished the house, brick by brick. The great walls, mellow tiles, windows and heavy doors together with all the fine carved stonework were torn down. Wood from the ceilings and the superb panelling were all put to the torch. The stone and bricks were scattered about the Island and by the time Maurice George Bissett died on 16 December 1821 all that remained of Knighton Gorges were a pair of stone gateposts.

The entrance to Knighton Gorges showing the loaves of bread on top of the pillars, which allegedly turn to griffins.

Sir Henry Englefield was to visit the house in 1800 and he described it in some detail: 'The principal front to the north is of the age of Elizabeth, irregular and broken by projections. The windows are large, divided by stone mullions; square headed and without any smaller arches in the angles of the lights; the general form very good, and the stone of which the whole house, except the chimneys, is built, is of an extremely fine grey tint. The west end of the house is enveloped in ivy which winds lightly round a tall stack of clustered chimneys, and embroiders with its deep green chutes the glowing yellow of the ancient mossy-tiled roof. This has been closely trimmed, injuring its beauty and giving a rather formal appearance. At the north-east angle of the house is a plain square tower of great strength and antiquity, in whose foundations there is a dungeon of considerable depth. Near this tower, part of a very handsome painted window remains, similar to windows in Arreton Church and the chapel at Swainston. This has been partly obliterated by the insertion of a

window of the same date as the north front. The south front has been modernised by sash windows, but the colour is good and two great gables remain uninjured

'The house contains several large and convenient rooms. Some have a handsome wainscot, probably contemporary with the north front. The drawing room on the first floor is spacious and handsome. A long gallery, low and ill lighted extends to the centre of the house, under the roof. No painted glass remains in the windows except one coat with the arms of Isabella the Forties, but this appears to be of a date much later than her time. A very ancient edifice, probably once a chapel, stands on the margin of the lake, and seems to be at least as old as the reign of Edward III.'

Today's visitors to the Island will only find a few crumbling walls, a grass mound and maybe a ruined stable – and still the ghosts are not settled.

In this sad region strange stories still linger. It was in the 1930s a young gentleman on a walking holiday knocked on the door of a house in Newchurch asking for lodgings for the night. As he was taking supper he told his hosts of an incident which had happened just prior to his arrival when he was nearly run down by a coach and horses making their way along the drive of the manor house. So annoyed was he that he walked on to the house in order to complain. He knocked repeatedly but no one answered although looking through the window he saw a fancy dress party in progress. Still no one heard his knock so he walked back along the drive and made his way to Newchurch. He then pointed out the position of the house on the map and from his description there was no doubt that he referred to Knighton Gorges which had been razed to the ground by Bissett a century earlier.

Even the stone gateposts seem to be haunted for many locals including some coach and taxi drivers claim to have seen the roundels known locally as 'loaves of bread' which surmount the top of the posts, turn into griffins, a cross between a hind part of a lion and the fore part of an eagle.

Still the mysteries linger on. When the house was demolished a bricked-up niche in one of the walls revealed a human skeleton and still more remains have been found in the lake. Human skeletons were found hidden in walls which seemed to be able to tell of the murderous deeds and events which resulted in the agonising screams which can still be heard at the dead of night; even to the sound and sight of a spectral hound, bleeding profusely from the treatment it had received from cruel masters.

Who ill-treated the hound? Who is the dark knight? Who is the headless horseman? Why does the manor house reappear on New Year's Eve? Where lie the dark secrets of Knighton Gorges?

Blue Lady of Nettlestone

DRIVING north towards the coast we reach the small village of Nettlestone. How this name originated no one is sure but we do know that a parcel of land in the area was granted to the Cluniac monks of Burgundy soon after the Norman Conquest.

It is to the promontory now known as Nodes Point where, long ago there was built a small farmhouse which, through the love and care of many owners, was converted into a beautiful mansion. Legend has it that at one time a secret passage led from this house to the nearby St Helen's Priory which stood in the fields beyond.

The monks having built the priory enjoyed and farmed the land around St Helen's for many years. It was not until foreign religious orders were banished from England by Henry V that the lands reverted to English hands when they lapsed to the crown. Today no remains exist of the original priory but the house has retained the name of The Priory.

We have little knowledge of ownership until the reign of Henry VI, when he decreed that the revenues were to be granted to Eton College.

Subsequently, during the reign of Edward IV, and on the occasion of his marriage to Elizabeth Woodville, the bursars of Eton College were granted the actual land. And so it was to remain until 1799 when the founder of the Grose-Smith family, Sir Grose Nash, purchased the property.

In 1927, it was purchased by a wealthy lady from America who became so enchanted with England that she was to adopt St George and the Dragon as her personal symbol, even to the extent of changing her name to St George. From then many interesting improvements were made. From France, she imported a porch and had it rebuilt stone by stone at The Priory. It is thought that this porch dates from the 14th century. True to form she added a sculptured figure of St George and the Dragon carved from different stone.

During the 130 years of occupation by the Grose-Smiths, hanging in the dining room was a portrait known as 'The Blue Lady'. It was of a smiling young girl, about 14 years old, with a canary perched on the first finger and thumb of her right hand and a little King Charles Spaniel dog sitting at her feet. The origin of this portrait is unknown as is the artist, but legend has it that the young girl, wearing a striking blue dress of the period died a short while after the

The main entrance to Nettlestone Priory Hotel, showing the Twelve Apostles and St George and the Dragon.

the company of her mother and grandmother paid a visit to Mrs St George and was to hear first-hand accounts of the many sightings and experiences from the new owner who said that her main difficulty was keeping servants. No sooner had one given notice and a replacement found, than they, too, would leave. It was extremely puzzling as she could get no satisfactory answer as to the reason for the constant change. However, when her faithful butler handed in his resignation she managed to gain an insight into the sudden departure of her staff. When finally persuaded to divulge his reasons for leaving, he said that the staff were petrified of the noises at night and described heart-rending cries as if a little child were crying and calling for her dog. He told Mrs St George with embarrassment that they could only take so much.

Apparently, the servants, on hearing the sound for the first time would try to find out what was happening – but on arrival, there would be nothing to see. Some of them, including the butler, heard soft childlike footsteps running past them.

Being an astute judge of character, Mrs St George had no doubt as to the credibility of the butler's explanation, but wanting independent evidence she began making inquiries among the local people and soon discovered that a ghostly girl did in fact haunt the house and surrounding area but could find out nothing about a ghostly dog. It was not until talking to the gardener who had

portrait was painted. How and why is a mystery, but since her death there has been much evidence of her ghost being seen, not only in the priory but in the grounds and nearby fields. In most sightings she is either playing with or calling for her little dog.

On talking to some of the local residents I was to learn that in about 1927 a distant relative of the Grose-Smiths, in

The little dog at Nettlestone Priory Hotel.

lived there for most of his life that she first heard mention of a stuffed dog. For most of his living memory it had been in a glass case over the stairs.

He pointed out that it had now gone having been sold with most of the contents of the old house. Had the presence of this stuffed dog any connection with the dog in the painting? Was the removal of the stuffed dog in any way connected with the ghost of the child, causing it to appear? Could the original dog be found and replaced? These questions and many others played upon Mrs St George's fertile imagination and assuming that there would be no great demand for such a curio, she placed an advertisement in the local newspaper. Much to her delight she had an immediate response and was able to purchase it back for the sum of one pound, triumphantly restoring it to its rightful place. Indeed, the apparition of the blue lady seemingly in distress and calling for her dog ceased.

Much later, one of the modern owners, Mr Kenneth Lee of Galleon Travel Association, tells of the time that someone, unaware of the story removed and deposited the stuffed dog into one of the cellars. Almost immediately the strange noises were heard again during the night. The next morning the dog was replaced and the ghostly noises soon ceased. The apparition of the girl, the Blue Lady of Nettlestone, still from time to time is seen, but in recent years is seemingly content. No running or crying. No calling for her lost dog, but apparently happy in her wanderings.

As for her portrait. It was inherited by Commander Douglas RN retired and was moved to his home in Sussex. It has been suggested that perhaps one day it will be returned to its original home and maybe the ghost of the blue lady will walk no more. However, I do not think the picture would make any difference, for if she could find no rest whilst it hung in the great hall, why should it make any difference if it were to be returned?

The present owners gave me permission to arrange for a photograph of the little dog and to remove it from the glass case for this purpose. My colleague gently lifted the well-preserved creature from the case and placed it on a cushion for the photograph. As he said subsequently." It was an odd experience handling such a famous creature for the first time in 200 years. Maybe the girl was the last living person to have held the little dog."

One thing is now certain. The pretty little King Charles Spaniel is now sealed back in the glass fronted case and hopefully will remain there for many more centuries. During my researches into the apparition of the blue lady and her little dog, I was to find a well written and informative account in *Ghosts of Hampshire and the Isle of Wight* by one of the most experienced and world renowned authorities on the subject, Peter Underwood.

The author pictured in the oak-panelled haunted room at Nettlestone Priory Hotel.

Return of a King

SOUTH of the Island capital, Newport, and situated just outside the village of Chillerton is Billingham Manor, the very epitome of the best in English architecture, standing as it does surrounded by the rolling countryside, with extensive views over Bleakdown.

In the mid-1920s Sir Shane Leslie and his wife rented the manor and learning about the many stories relating to the house in connection with the attempted escape of King Charles I, who was held captive in nearby Carisbrooke Castle, Sir Shane decided to search for any missing clues which would throw light on the legend that the King did, in fact, visit Billingham Manor and was concealed there for a time.

This legend has it that His Majesty hid himself in a compartment in the drawing room, concealed by a sliding panel. It is also said the hiding place was so narrow and uncomfortable, that the King chose to return to his confinement at Carisbrooke Castle, rather than to suffer the agonies of such a confined space whilst he waited in vain for a ship to take him to France.

In fact, Sir Shane did find a small secret coffin-shaped compartment. Could this have been the King's hiding place?

Whether or not there had been noisy apparitions prior to the finding of the hiding place I have been unable to ascertain, but it is documented that from the day of its discovery, heavy footsteps and metallic sounds, like swords being dragged over stone floors, were heard and at one time an extremely distressed housemaid reported seeing a man who walked across the room and made his exit through the outer wall.

Very early one morning in 1928 these mysterious noises were so loud that the whole household was disturbed. Sir Shane and Lady Leslie both got up to investigate and as they left their room were joined by the rest of the occupants of the house. The noises seemed to emanate from the drawing room and it was not without apprehension that Sir Shane led them in their quest to ascertain who or what was causing the disturbance. On arrival they saw a faint light shining through the cracks surrounding the sliding panel. Sir Shane advanced and slid back the panel. The brilliance from within was similar to phosphorescent light, which they described as if they had momentarily looked directly at the sun. As their vision cleared all present in the room reported seeing the severed head of King Charles I staring at them from the recess. Each person swore that it was looking directly at them. The was no mistaking the apparition, the soft ringlets of hair, the pointed beard and the pitiful look of agony in its eyes.

As they all watched, too petrified to move, and with the glow slowly subsiding the spectre gradually faded, leaving them staring into the empty coffin shaped hiding place. During the course of further research into the history of Billingham Manor, Sir Shane was to discover diaries belonging to a former owner, which described in exact detail a spectre matching that which the household had witnessed.

What research did show was that on the same day the severed head had been seen at Billingham in 1928, a prisoner had been executed in Newport prison. Maybe the King, only too aware of the distress suffered by those who are doomed to die, is drawn back into the twilight world on such occasions.

J.B.Priestley was to take up residence at Billingham Manor in 1933 and there wrote some of his famous works. On one occasion his son, Robert, remarked that he was continually being watched by a little woman, but his father, although assuring him that there was no woman in the house was unable to pacify him. There are reports of this small, smiling woman visiting Billingham Manor on many occasions. Sometime later Priestley's publisher, on taking his leave at the front door asked the author to thank his housekeeper. This remark was to shock Priestley for he knew that no woman was present in the house. Another report made by a guest stated that a frightening apparition materialised on the famous Inigo Jones staircase.

Another apparition which has been seen at Billingham is that of a lady dressed in grey. Her appearances are often accompanied by violent disturbances as if the house were at the epicentre of a small earthquake.

One spectre observed by a former Duchess of Argyle was that of a monk like figure dressed in a brown habit. This apparition was accompanied by sounds akin to heavy boxes or crates being dragged across the stone floor together with heavy footsteps. Recently, music has been heard accompanied by the unmistakable scent of the madonna lily.

Among other stories attached to Billingham Manor is that back in the realms of yesteryear, one of the beautiful Worsley daughters was engaged to a neighbouring squire. However, it was to a visiting Frenchman that she lost her heart. It is said that on the front lawns of the house the English squire and the Frenchman fought a duel which resulted in the Frenchman receiving a fatal injury. Legend has it that his ghost still haunts the manor and at certain times this ghostly dual can be seen taking place.

To enlarge slightly on this story we return to the year 1722 when the rebuilding of Billingham Manor took place and it passed to one of the sons of the Worsley family of Appuldurcombe on his marriage to Miss Leigh from Shorwell. As was the custom at that time marriages were arranged for the advancement of families and little thought was given to the wishes of the bride. In this particular case, the young Miss Leigh was madly in love with a nobleman from France. After her marriage she would secretly meet her lover; but the inevitable happened and Worsley was to come upon them in the walled garden enjoying a lovers' embrace and challenged the Frenchman to a duel in the grounds of the manor. Both contestants in this deadly duel fought hard but alas, the Frenchman received a mortal wound. Worsley forbade his wife to leave the confines of the Manor and it is believed that the apparition of the grey lady seen at Billingham is that of the unhappy wife accompanied by the scent of the 'flower of mourning' the madonna lily.

It has been said that the present owners Mr and Mrs Spencer-Forbes still hear and encounter these mysteries, from the perfume of the lily, to many strange sounds and apparitions of men and women who, by their costume appear to belong to the 16th or 17th centuries. Clocks in the house advance several hours for no apparent reason and at other times mysterious music fills the air, and so hauntings at Billingham continue, even to this day.

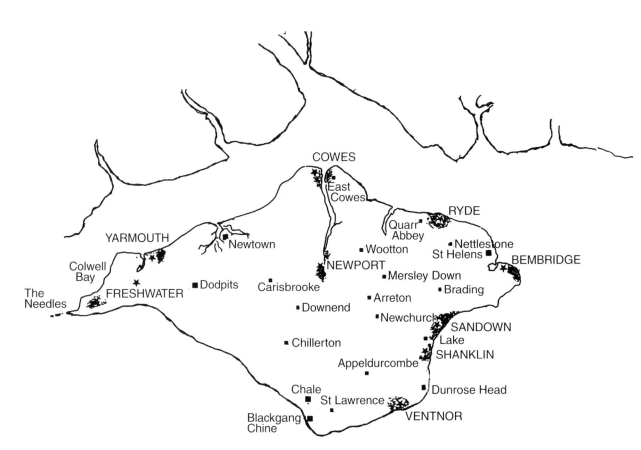

ISLE OF WIGHT

Mad Michael Morey of Downend

IN THE annals of Island crime the following story must surely be the most brutal ever to come to light.

In the year 1735 Michael Morey, an extremely vain woodcutter, was growing old. His back was bent from years of swinging his axe against the oak and elm of the Island forests and resentment smouldered each time he saw his young handsome grandson.

The boy had recently inherited money and as Michael dragged himself back to his cottage he found that the grandson was again late in bringing his meal. As he waited, jealous hatred welled up inside him.

When eventually his grandson arrived, old Morey was sullen, not caring if he spoke or not. The lad could not understand his grandfather's bad temper as he vented his anger by saying that he had spent his whole life hewing wood to earn gold for his master and all he got out of his labours was copper.

The boy laughed and Michael Morey went berserk. Grabbing his axe that had a blade sharp enough to slice through heartwood of hard oak, he brought it down upon his grandson. As the blade bit into flesh and bone, blood oozed on to the earthen floor, staining the walls and flagstones around the fire.

Realising the terrible deed he had just committed, old Morey, threw his axe upon the dead boy, desperately gathered brushwood to fill the room; then setting fire to the brushwood, watched as the flames consumed the cottage, burning their way through the lath and plaster ceilings and reaching the thatch above. As the fire crackled under a cloud of smoke that whispered through the reeded roof, Morey knew that it would not have had time to consume the body of the unfortunate boy, but with a large explosive sound the ceiling and roof caved in falling on to the body and as he watched he thought his crime would be well and truly covered.

As the smoke began to clear, the horror rose within him, for where he had hoped to weep unsuspecting for the death of his grandson and his lost home, there, by the hearth was the unmistakable body of the mutilated boy and the blood red flagstones and walls. Laying by the side of the body was Michael Morey's axe.

Fleeing in terror down the lane, Morey hid in a small hollow, trembling with fear. Meanwhile, his daughter, noticing smoke coming from the direction of her father's house, set out to investigate, only to find the ghastly remains of her son.

The Hare and Hounds, Downend. In the lounge is housed the gibbet on which Micheal Morey was hanged. This is the hostelry in which Dr and Mrs White sought refuge after their terrifying experience (see *Another Time – Another Place?*).

Magistrates were informed and they called out the military and the manhunt began. Not many hours later the trembling Michael Morey was hauled from the hollow, charged with the hideous crime of murder and taken to Winchester to be tried at the assizes.

As the terrible facts of the crime unfolded, people in the court fainted at the thought of the sheer brutality that had been wrought on the unsuspecting boy. The murderous woodcutter was found guilty and sentenced to be publicly hanged at Winchester, his body sealed in an iron cage and taken back to the Isle of Wight to hang from a gibbet at the spot known as Gallows Hill at Downend. The corpse in its iron frame

was left to hang for all to see for many months in this desolate spot until the villagers of Arreton petitioned for its removal, stating that it was an offence to both eye and nostril. The petition was granted and the body was buried in an unmarked grave.

The lane in which Michael Morey lived is now known as Burnt House Lane and the site of the gibbet as Morey's Mount. Opposite Morey's Mount is an inn called the Hare and Hounds, the inn mentioned in chapter three.

When I was there about two years ago I was shown one of the crossbeams made out of the old gibbet and clearly to be seen was the notch cut to hold the rope and its vile burden. Beside it was inscribed the date of Morey's execution.

In the book *Ghosts of The Isle of Wight* by Steadman and Anker is a quote which reads. "I was cycling along Burnt House Lane one night just after the war. It was moonlight and the road was clear, so I was surprised when I suddenly saw a man walking towards me near the lane that leads to Great East Standen. He hadn't been there a moment before. I thought he must have stepped out from the hedgerows. When I got closer I could see he was wearing some sort of leather leggings and a leather jerkin, but the rest of his clothes were ragged. The oddest thing was his hat, a floppy black thing with a feather or two stuck into it. I thought he had a shotgun over his shoulder but when I reached him I saw it was a big axe with a piece of cloth tied around the blade. I glanced back the second I had passed him, he looked so odd – but he had gone. I couldn't believe it. He had just vanished. It wasn't possible. That old bike fair shook, the speed I pedalled back to Newport..."

One evening in 1964, Mr and Mrs John Paine of Sandown had been visiting their son at Pan Estate, Newport. It was late evening and raining hard as they drove along Burnt House Lane intending, on arrival at Downend, to drive home via Arreton. Sitting in his comfortable, well lit terraced house John related to me the happenings of what he described as 'that terrible night'.

"We had just negotiated the narrowest part of Burnt House Lane when suddenly out of the lane which leads to Great East Standen Manor emerged a man running fast. I braked hard to miss him stopping just inches away from him. He seemed not to notice that we were even there. As he turned to face us we could see through the rain-spotted windscreen that instead of eyes, there were just black empty sockets. The beam of our headlights was able to pick out his face quite clearly. It was for the most part just a skull, but with strips of what looked like rotting flesh hanging from it. In his hand was a large woodman's axe. I turned to Joan, my wife, with a mixture of disbelief and horror to see if she had witnessed the same sight. I could tell from her face that she had. Turning once more to look through the windscreen, the road was completely clear. I was at that point unable to speak a word to my wife and resumed the journey home, but I don't think I could possibly have been travelling more than about ten miles an hour. It was not until we were approaching the Fighting Cocks cross roads that Joan suddenly screamed and this brought me back more to my senses so we hurried home. Later that evening I had to call our doctor who gave my wife a sedative. I think it will be many years before we can come to terms with what we had witnessed."

In all my ghost hunting and researches into other people's sightings of apparitions I confess that this ranks as one of the most horrendous reports I have heard. Is it any wonder then that Michael Morey should find no rest after his foul deed and the punishment meted out to him?

The Hospital That Wouldn't Die

A N UNUSUAL geological feature occurs along part of the southern coast line of the Isle of Wight. Travelling to this spot we find ourselves on a very large shelf, which although jutting out to sea, is protected fully by the cliffs above. The whole area is called The Undercliff.

Here, it was decided to build a hospital for patients suffering essentially with chest complaints. Known as Ventnor Hospital this building, with its long airy

Seaward view of Ventor Chest Hospital.

corridors and wards facing the sea, was to serve the Island community for many decades until it closed in 1964.

There then followed much speculation as to what possible use the 22 acre site could be put. Discussion took place at high level during the next five years and in 1969 it was agreed that the site would be used for a Botanical Garden.

Demolition work on the hospital building commenced in 1969 and all went well until the contractors reached the old operating theatre. It was then that strange and inexplicable things began to happen.

Mr Roy Dore, a park superintendent now retired, said. "After what happened I have an open mind on ghosts and poltergeists. We had experts down to look into it but there was no logical explanation. We had to knock down the old hospital and all went well until we reached the old operating theatre. That seemed to have a mind of its own. It resisted every attempt to demolish it. Whether it was machine or man – they suffered. First a bulldozer was wrecked when three large slabs of masonry fell on it. Luckily the driver was unhurt but he was badly shaken. Then the contractors brought in a crane with a heavy metal ball. All that happened was that the steel cable connected to the ball kept snapping. Then they used a tractor, putting a large cable round the walls in an attempt to pull them down that way. The tractor was retired, damaged. It was all very embarrassing but we left it alone and started demolishing at the other side

of the operating theatre. It meant, of course, that we were having troubles with people entering a half demolished site and more for their safety we brought in a security company but they had problems. When they turned their dogs loose, they just cringed away and nothing could persuade them to enter the area."

Roy Dore went on to tell of many other incidents that occurred when trying to tear down the old operating theatre, but again the heavy plant always withdrew, damaged. I was amazed when Roy, who was then and is still now considered an extremely level-headed man, continued, "In the end we brought in two men to knock it down by hand. One day when having their meal break they swore that a ghost appeared beside them. They both suffered a breakdown. Another workman saw a ghost and he too was sent home in a state of extreme nervousness. Yet another time, a surveyor, peering through his theodolite reported seeing two figures which then vanished. These incidents were to bring the psychic research people to our door. They arrived with electrical ghost tracing equipment, and slept in their cars and in shelters."

At last, the operating theatre was levelled and it was hoped that this would put and end to the troubles but – how wrong they were.

A trench was dug across the site into which was laid heavy duty electrical cable to serve what is now the Botanical Gardens cafeteria. After many mishaps the job was completed and tests were carried out on the cable which was buried under what is now the car park. All seemed to be well – that was until it was time for the cafeteria to open. There was no electricity. Work then started to dig up the newly surfaced car park to unearth the cable. Nothing was amiss until the electricians reached the site of the old operating theatre. There they found to their horror that the buried cable had been torn into shreds approximately two feet six inches long. Sections of it were kept and placed in the gardener's store as proof that something strange had happened and there they remain to this day.

Working with Roy Dore at the time was Alan Taylor, who also reported seeing an apparition which he likened to the figure in the television advertisement for Sandeman Port, viz, a long cloak, wide brimmed hat and lace up boots. He said it was crossing the old tennis courts but on going closer to investigate, it disappeared.

Roy Dore went on to explain that five services of exorcism were carried out in the gardens before the late Earl Mountbatten officially opened them in 1972.

During the course of my investigation I was to read a report by Clive Barton who at that time was a reporter on the *Isle of Wight County Press*. He interviewed Mr Simon Goodenough, at that time the curator of Ventnor Botanical Gardens. Here, with kind permission of the *County Press*, I quote:

"I thought it was rubbish, but then one night I went to get into my car after finishing work and this man approached me – he just seemed to appear from nowhere.

"He said, 'You're new here, aren't you?' I was in a hurry to get away so I just agreed, and got into my car. Just as I drove off, he said 'Not like me – I've been in hospital here for almost a year now'. Simon Goodenough said 'I had driven a little way when I suddenly realised what he had said. The hospital had long since been demolished. The hackles rose on my neck – I am convinced he was unnatural'."

Later, I was to meet one of the nurses who worked in the hospital, Mrs M.Pugsley, who was to tell me about incidents which took place near the operating theatre in the years prior its closure. Nurses would report footsteps in empty wards, taps which inexplicably turned themselves on and other weird phenomena. I asked her if she had personally witnessed anything strange and she told me:

"We nurses had a small room near the operating theatre which we used when on night shift as a place where we could have a lay down during our rest break. You must realise at the time I was only a young trainee nurse and liked my sleep. This particular night when it was time for my break I decided to go and have a nap on the couch provided. Being quite cold I took the hospital cat with me. He was a big, affectionate, fluffy Persian type cat who liked to be cuddled. The cat and I had been laying there for

`The site of Ventor Chest Hospital, now occupied by the Botanical Gardens.

approximately half an hour when I was aroused with a start. I did not know what it was, but I knew that something was wrong and had the feeling that someone was watching me. I can't remember being scared, but I certainly had a feeling that 'icy fingers' were running up and down my back. The cat, who was in my arms, suddenly seemed to swell to twice his size as his fur stood on end and his tail bushed. In the moonlight I could see that a dark shape was standing in the corner of the room. I cannot say if it was a man or a woman. It was just a dark misty shape. Needless to say, I soon grabbed my hat and shoes and beat a hasty retreat, the cat yelling and going before me. It was many nights before either me or the cat ventured anywhere near that room."

One thing became apparent to me. Mr Dore, a well-respected member of the community, Mr Goodenough, a man with a scientific background who had served 12 years in the prodigious Royal Botanical Gardens at Kew and who commanded respect throughout his profession, Mr Taylor, the man in charge of the gardens, and then Mrs Pugsley, who finished her career as a nursing sister. Surely they are not all wrong?

How also is it possible that electrical cable can be so systematically torn to shreds when careful examination of the car park surfacing material and earth under which it had been buried revealed no interference or movement?

Let us also consider the position of the Botanical Gardens, a place where bananas, limes, lemon and orange trees grow outside with no artificial heat, yet in a climate not recognised for such feats of nature. Among more familiar species from abroad there are many rarities and oddities which thrive including cyclads from the Far East which were a popular diet of the dinosaur. I know of nowhere else in the country where such a plant grows in the open. In a place such as this, is it any wonder that spectres from the paranormal do exist and that both men and machinery were thwarted in their attempt to alter the landscape?

On my last visit to the gardens I could not help but think of the headline in the local paper some years ago.

'Everything in the garden is lovely, except history of hauntings.'

Smoking Ghost of Golden Hill

WE cannot mention a fort unless we take our minds back to our childhood, when forts conjured up a picture of knights in shining armour, or even Cowboys and Indians. Many forts, however, were constructed as late as the early 19th century.

One such establishment on the Isle of Wight is Golden Hill Fort in Freshwater. Despite Wellington's victory at the Battle of Waterloo in 1815, Lord Palmerston still had doubts about the safety of Spithead, the entrance to Portsmouth Harbour, then the home of the British Fleet.

Aerial view of Golden Hill Fort, Freshwater during the 1984 restoration period.

The inner courtyard of Golden Hill Fort showing the Lord Palmerston and Sheila Hughes' Colonnade Tearooms.

In 1859 the French were to launch *La Gloire* the world's first iron-clad steam warship. Panic reigned to such an extent that Lord Palmerston's government were to set up the Royal Commission on the Defences of the United Kingdom. The Commission's report in 1860 recommended that Portsmouth should be protected on all sides, thus making a safe refuge for the fleet.

Situated as it is, the Isle of Wight lies across the approaches to the harbour and Southampton Water. Once having taken care of the main approaches, Palmerston had to look at what may be described as the 'back door approach', The Needles Channel, so he decided that a line of forts should be built on the Island to protect this narrow channel. At the same time a fort would be built inland, thus ensuring that the other forts would not be vulnerable to attacks from overland. Large guns were to be housed on the high battlements, thus giving a field of fire to cover all inland approaches.

This fort at Golden Hill, completed in 1872, was, throughout its history, never called upon to fire a shot in anger. During peacetime it served as a garrison for many units of the armed services and also acted as a small military hospital.

It was here that the survivors of HMS *Gladiator* (as mentioned in the chapter Of Phantom Ships and Sailors) were cared for after their rescue.

During World War One, one of the regiments stationed at Golden Hill Fort was the Duke of Cornwall's Light Infantry, with over 30,000 officers and men passing through before being posted overseas.

During World War Two it was again put to use as a training establishment and was used as a dormitory for troops awaiting the D-Day landings. At the cessation of hostilities it was handed over to the Royal Army Transport Corps as a barracks. It finally closed in 1962 and was to lay dormant until sold in 1969 as an industrial site. In 1984 restoration work began and Golden Hill Fort was, for the first time in its history, to open its doors to visitors.

At this point I would like to make a statement. It was an incident which occurred at Golden Hill Fort which first turned my thoughts towards the paranormal. In the summer of 1989 I opened a small jewellery and gift shop in one of the units in the Victorian Corridor at the fort which by this time had been converted into a craft and retail centre with other parts reflecting its historical and military connections.

In the evening after closing my unit and coping with the 101 little jobs associated with a seasonal business, I would often sense the pungent smell of aromatic tobacco. At first I gave little thought to it, presuming there was someone from an adjoining shop also working late.

Victorian corridor of Golden Hill Fort.

One evening, with the distinct aroma of the tobacco still in my mind, I mentioned it to the manager Ivor Allison and his wife Jill. They informed me that, far from it being caused by another shop keeper, I had been watched over by the spirit of a long departed resident of the fort. Ivor described the aroma with an authenticity which shook me, for it was an unusual blend. He explained that it was thought that the apparition, although not appearing to me had in fact been present. "It is thought to be the ghost of the sergeant," he said. "As far as we are able to ascertain, two men were on foot patrol on the battlements. The sergeant of the guard, a kindly man, on making his rounds discovered their absence. Without reporting this he decided to visit the local hostelry where he found the two absentees. Admonishing them he ordered them to return to their posts at once saying that he would speak to them later. After finishing his rounds he returned to the battlements. What was said we do not know, but it was alleged that a fight ensued and the sergeant either slipped or was thrown down the spiral staircase, breaking his neck. It is said that no charges were brought owing to the fact that there was no evidence that he was either pushed or thrown, but many times since that day the aroma of his tobacco smoke is still evident in the Victorian Corridor. Incidentally, it is known that the sergeant's tobacco is not available in this country, nor has it been for many years."

Fascinated by what Ivor had told me I inquired about any other paranormal occurrences in the establishment. It was Jill who was to continue the conversation. "Well, we have got one well authenticated ghost, that of the young soldier who was executed here by hanging. The trap door which was purposely built for the execution is still to be seen."

I asked Jill if she was in possession of any further details. It was Jill and Ivor between them who eventually told me the story.

It appeared that a young soldier had in his possession the plans of the fortifications, and, deciding to make the most of it, tried to sell them to the French. Luckily for the security of the Navy his bid failed and he was arrested, duly court-martialled at Golden Hill Fort, sentenced to death and executed. The spectre of this unfortunate soldier is often seen in the area which is now the Lord Palmerston pub situated next to the entrance tunnel. Alan Burgess, the then tenant of the Lord Palmerston, was to tell me of the time he saw the apparition standing in the passageway leading to the kitchens. He seemed to be smiling and when Alan appeared, slowly walked away melting into the surrounding brickwork. Another time, Alan, and others saw the uniformed spectre leaning against the front door frame. Recently, two couples entered the bar and proceeded to sit at a vacant table at the far end. The two men went up to the bar and ordered the drinks but before they could be served they were joined by their ladies, one of whom had become extremely pallid and said that she would have to leave as there was a very strong psychic presence in the bar. They left without purchasing their refreshments. Towards the end of the summer of 1990 I was sitting in my unit when the door burst open and Sheila Hughes, the proprietor of the Colonnade Tea Rooms situated on the opposite side of the tunnel entrance to the Lord Palmerston, staggered into my room. I can only describe her state as one of extreme agitation. I felt she was near to becoming hysterical. Fearing that I would be unable to cope I called for assistance from another shopkeeper. Fortunately, Sheila was able to regain her composure with the aid of a strong coffee and related the fact that she had been clearing the cups and saucers from the tables and placing them in the pantry prior to washing up. She then decided to go into the back storeroom which

entailed walking through a short, narrow passageway. As she entered the passage her way was obstructed by an apparition of a man in uniform, the style or age of the uniform she was uncertain of. She stated. "I know I was being silly, but I think it was more the shock of seeing someone standing there, more in the back room than in the passageway, that I just panicked."

Knowing Sheila to be an extremely level-headed person, not only well respected within the community, but also a volunteer driver for the local Tennyson Ambulance and certainly not a woman given to flights of fancy, I could only take her story seriously. I offered to accompany her back to the Tea Rooms, an offer which she readily accepted. I searched the place thoroughly but could find nothing amiss.

There are two other incidents which occurred as far as I could ascertain within the fort precincts. One was of a sailor in uniform dating from the turn of the century. It is thought that it could only be one of those unfortunate members of the crew of the *Gladiator* who was saved from the wreck but subsequently died in Golden Hill Fort Military Hospital.

The second is more rather ongoing and here I would like to quote one more paragraph from Ivor Allison who has lived and worked within the confines of Golden Hill Fort from the start of its restoration in 1984.

"At one time, when locking the units open to the public I would start at the spiral staircase where the unfortunate sergeant met his untimely end. Firstly, completing my round of the battlements until arriving back to the staircase and descending it, thus making my way along the balconies to the Victorian Corridor, ensuring that all lights were out and all doors closed. The hair on my neck many times I am certain, was perpendicular as I felt a presence tracing my steps. I can assure you I neither had an inquisitive enough nature to turn and look. Neither, might I add, the courage. But my footsteps quickened the nearer I got to finishing."

Having spent three seasons at Golden Hill Fort I have no doubt as to the presence of unidentified spectre there, nor do I doubt the truthfulness of my fellow workers who heard, saw and smelt strange things.

Ivor and Jill Allison, former managers of Freshwater's Golden Hill Fort.

Mad Monk of Appuldurcombe

APPULDURCOMBE House near Wroxall had a chequered history and during its long life has been a priory of the Abbey of Montebourg in Normandy, and following the suppression of alien houses was granted to the Nun Minoresses Without Aldgate. It is a house which Sir Robert Worsley boasted of having razed to the ground, but the Worsley motto was 'Ut Sursum Desuper' – 'I Swoop To Rise Again' and the new house was to pass to the Earl of Yarborough's wife. It was sold in 1855. The Revd Pound ran an academy for young gentlemen there before the Benedictines of Solesmes. The house that had entertained such people as Henry VIII and Thomas Cromwell was destroyed by a land mine in 1942 and is now a roofless ruin.

This house at one time was the home of the mighty Worsley family and the inn at the nearby village of Wroxall is named after the great Sir Richard Worsley.

Prior to the Worsley family owning the house it was a refuge for a group of Benedictine monks who had been expelled from their Abbey at Solesmes in France and during their stay at Appuldurcombe House it is said that one of the brothers became mentally ill and knowing that the local people would associate mental illness with the Devil and evil, the Abbot kept him hidden deep inside the great house during the hours of daylight, only letting him out at night. Grateful to be in the clean night air the brother would run and walk harmlessly through the fields and lanes near Appuldurcombe. At first some of the villagers who were out late at night would be startled by the sudden appearance of this happy monk running and skipping through the lanes. The Abbot, in order to allay their possible fear, gave the mad monk a hand bell so that all knew he was there; and happy in his state of madness the monk would wander through the night, slowly and joyfully ringing his bell as he meandered on his nocturnal pleasures.

The villagers were not unduly put out by the ringing of the bell and thought it a small price to pay to keep the monk happy.

A few years after the monks moved to Appuldurcombe House the mad monk died. But alas, even then he could find no rest, for during the hours of darkness many have seen his hooded figure and heard his bell as he played in the mead-

Appuldurcombe House.

ows and lanes near the village. Even to this day there are folk who have reported his spectre about the lanes of Appuldurcombe. At one time in the not too distant past, the monks of Quarr Abbey were also to spend some time at Appuldurcombe House whilst awaiting completion of their new Abbey on the outskirts of Ryde.

The first Abbey at Quarr was consecrated by Henry de Blois over 800 years ago but all that remains of it today is the one ruined grey wall.

De Blois arrived on the Island for the consecration of the great Abbey on New Year's Day, the Feast of Fools. It is claimed that The Feast of Fools was directed by the Lord of Misrule and the monks would dress as women and sing bawdy songs, burning their old shoes as incense and using the altar as a table from which they ate puddings and sausages. It is believed that this is a pagan ceremony left over from the past festivals of Saturnalia and Bacchanalia.

After the death of Richard the Lion Heart, his mother Eleanor was restrained at the old Quarr Abbey for many years and would take her lonely walks in the area which now bears the name Eleanor's Walk. She loved the place so much that she gave orders that upon her death it was here that she wished to be interred; when she died her body was placed in a solid gold coffin, brought to Quarr where an underground tunnel leading to a tomb beneath her favourite spot had been prepared. A golden gate was sealed by magic spells and the entry became lost in antiquity.

During the reign of Queen Victoria a concerted effort was made to trace the last resting place of Eleanor. A tunnel leading to a tomb was discovered, but alas, no golden gates, no golden coffin – not even a body was found. Whether that was the last resting place of Queen Eleanor there is no way of knowing, but what has been reported over the centuries and still to this day are sightings of the unhappy Queen taking her lonely walks along what is now known as Eleanor's Walk.

It was at Ryde, that I was to speak to David Silver, a local businessman who one day in September 1975 had stopped his car in the lane leading to Quarr Abbey and taken a walk with his dog along a route which led him past the old Abbey grounds. It was a warm autumn evening and he was not wearing a coat, but suddenly he felt a chill, as if he had just opened a refrigerator. His dog, a Jack Russell, a breed not known for their timidness, cowered and trembled against his leg. Then about 40 yards in front of where he was standing he saw the spectre of a woman, dressed in costume similar to pictures he had seen of ladies of the court at the time of Queen Eleanor. As quickly as it appeared, so it vanished and the air regained its autumn warmth, but it was some days before Trixie, the Jack Russell, was to recover fully. Today there stands at Quarr a magnificent red brick Abbey bearing no resemblance either to the old Abbey building or to their misguided feast days. In the early 1980s the then secretary stated that he had considerable doubts as to whether Henry II could have afforded golden gates and a golden coffin for Eleanor, and in any case, there is no historical evidence that Queen Eleanor was ever buried at Quarr. If she was not, then for whom were the tunnel and the tomb built, and who was this apparition which was seen by my friend David Silver and his little dog Trixie and so many others over the centuries?

The King's Chamber

LOWER St James Street is situated in Newport, Isle of Wight. Running through Hunnyhill it eventually leads to the main Cowes road. With its Victorian terraced houses, most of which are now used for offices, a few shops at the southern end, Lower St James Street is of very little interest architecturally or historically. However, at its junction with Lugley Street there still stands the ancient building which once housed the King James I Grammar School constructed in 1618.

Thirty years later, King Charles I was taken from Carisbrooke Castle to this building prior to the signing of the Treaty of Newport. One of the large oak-panelled rooms was used for the series of meetings which lasted for 60 days and in which the Monarch was carefully examined as to his intentions for the country. His comfortable sleeping quarters and those for his servants constituted the rooms above. Later that year, on 30 November, His Majesty was arrested after the negotiations with Parliament failed when he refused to accept the terms offered by Cromwell. Charles I was seized from these same rooms whence he was escorted by the army to London where he was eventually tried and executed.

The beginning of 1649 saw the building returned to its original use as a school and since that time many generations of Island and Mainland children have received a high standard of education within the walls of this historic Grammar School. Not long after the death of Charles I and the subsequent visits to the Island of his son, Charles II, many tales began emanating from the boys at the school. Tales of the room which had been occupied by Charles I becoming simultaneously cold, yet clammy even on the hottest of days, together with loud footsteps in the corridor and sounds of soldiers being brought rapidly to attention. These stories quickly became a favourite talking point in homes, taverns and wherever there happened to be a group of people, but were soon dismissed as either 'the vivid imagination of schoolboys' or a practical joke. Either way, conversations about the Ghosts of King James School virtually ceased as did the reports themselves, although some working-class families who, at the time were unable to afford education, would be wary when in the vicinity of the building.

Although these phenomena were experienced by many schoolboys over 316 years, very little was reported or even documented until after 1963 when the building was decommissioned as a school. Five years later the walls once again rang with the voices of children when it became Newport's Youth Cen-

**King James I
Grammar
School,
Newport, Isle of
Wight, now
Newport Youth
Centre.**

tre and, after a series of reported para-normal incidents I was able to meet Youth leader, Graham Dove.

He informed me that during the first few months of the life of the Youth Centre, some of the young members who had heard vague mentions of the haunting asked if they could instigate a project, thereby endeavouring to prove the authenticity of the story and find out whether or not these ghostly supernatural phenomena really happened.

Most of the youngsters were under 16, so after obtaining permission from parents and ascertaining the suitability of the youngsters involved to take part in such an experiment, Graham raised the idea at his next Youth Leaders meeting. As a result, one of the leaders volunteered to spend the night in the two rooms originally occupied by the king during his stay. He sensed very little downstairs in the oak-panelled room in which Charles I was questioned about his intentions, but reported a different and rather more serious story about the upstairs room used by the monarch as his bedroom, and the room from which he was eventually seized and arrested.

The report given by the assistant youth leader left Graham Dove in no doubt as to the authenticity of the centuries old reports. The young leader had experienced what he termed as 'supernatural activity' which was centred in and around the bedroom and out in the corridor. Although during the height of a hot summer with daytime temperatures averaging 27°C and the temperature at 30 minutes past midnight not much below 15°C, the room became extremely cold, clammy and uncomfortable. Checking the thermometer, he saw that it had not changed one iota. The temperature still read 15°C. He then heard voices and footsteps in the corridor outside. Describing the sounds as a general hubbub he said it resembled what he presumed would be the sounds of guards being changed. Opening the door and wondering just what would meet his eyes he saw – nothing; at the same time the sounds ceased abruptly.

Though he was brave enough to stay until next morning he was visibly concerned by the experience and cast doubts on the wisdom of allowing all but a few of the older members to stay – and then only if accompanied by leaders or parents.

The result was a series of organised so-called Fright Nights as most of the young people concerned were still intrigued, especially after the report of the experiences of the assistant leader. One of the girls told me "These activities proved a little scary, but extremely popular."

Although none of the children would ever spend the night on the premises, a 16-year-old lad related these facts to me which he said could be authenticated by other young members and leaders.

"We were clearing up late one night and happened to be in the room where King Charles once stayed. Strangely enough it was not one of the fright nights so we were not particularly bothered at the time about the ghosts and the noises and all that. Suddenly, there was

a drop in temperature. The room became cold and yet it seemed damp – like a warm sort of damp if you know what I mean. We were all sweating. There were about four of us and we all felt the same including one of our leaders. Then I felt something brush past me and whatever it was brushed past my girlfriend who was standing next to me. She tried to grab my arm but couldn't move. She said she opened her mouth to try to yell, but nothing seemed to come out. I know I didn't hear her. The thing went past us and we heard footsteps going out the door. We all heard sounds in the corridor like soldiers on parade and jumping to attention. We all rushed to the door and looked out but there was nothing at all. As we did this the noises stopped and the room warmed up again."

Asked if he was scared he said that he was at the time, but it wouldn't stop him going up there again. "But," he quickly added, "My girlfriend wouldn't go anywhere near the room – even with me!"

Others reported seeing figures moving around in the room which was lit with dim and flickering candles. These were often seen late at night by passers by when the centre was closed, and of course, in the same first floor bedroom. Whether this is just imagination or not I have no way of knowing as the story originally came from the 18-year-old sister of one of the members.

It is quite certain however that another spectre thought to be concerned with the school is that of a neatly dressed woman in dark blue who is regularly seen walking along Lugley Street and turning into the gate of the building. She is known locally as the Mauve Lady but there is very little information obtainable. It is thought she may have been employed at some stage by the school authorities as a matron or housekeeper.

It is evident that something happens periodically in that fateful first floor bedroom although it is impossible to ascertain that it is anything to do with King Charles. Some say that it is little wonder that the result of his visit to the Isle of Wight will not allow his troubled spirit to rest in peace. His treatment here was nothing but respectful, but the outcome is not the most savoury story in British history.

King Charles or not, truth or imagination, one thing is certain. Throughout the years there have been many reported spectral sightings in this area.

Phantom Gardener of St Lawrence Dene

FOR many years, standing proudly and built on three levels into the St Lawrence Undercliff, the beautiful house, St Lawrence Dene was owned by a succession of private individuals until being utilised by the then Isle of Wight County Council as a nursing home for the elderly and run by the Island's Social Services.

Although comfortable and extremely popular, it was never a great success as this type of residential home for a number of basic reasons. It is not difficult to imagine the frustration of the staff who were required to transport meals to three levels and keep them hot or to escort residents from the bottom level to the top level where was situated the main entrance leading directly on to the main road. This presented yet another hazard.

Eventually in the late 1980s the council closed St Lawrence Dene. The house remained empty for two years until being purchased by a private company, the upper level being used as a private nursing home and the other two levels and attached bungalow either sold or let for ordinary accommodation.

This weird tale was reported to me by someone who became a resident at St Lawrence Dene when it was still owned by the council. It involved certain happenings which may then, and even in retrospect, be seen as a protest by the ghost of an elderly lady resident of the nursing home who had long since departed this life. Her hobby, maybe even passion, had been gardening, and as such she was allowed, and even positively encouraged, to spend much of her time tending the gardens of the Dene. But now another gentleman with a similar passion for horticulture had taken her place and, even worse, had very little business to be a resident of St Lawrence Dene anyway.

Allow me to explain. As a boy, John Fuller found the process of learning extremely difficult. He was the sort of lad who could handle pretty well any manual task after having been shown once or twice. In respect of gardens, he was part of them, a natural, not only in the field of landscaping and design, but, without having the ability to read any planting or tending instructions would be able at a glance to plant at the correct time, diagnose and cure diseases of plants and shrubs and be able generally to live well out of his natural gift of possessing an affinity with nature. Although I personally knew John, I never knew much of his background which appears to have been shrouded in a little mystery. I presumed that his parents had both died when he was quite young. I am reasonably convinced that he lived with relatives who subsequently may have died or even moved away, but John was always reticent to discuss his earlier life and I was not prepared to press the subject. Whatever the facts, I was surprised one day when he announced his intention of moving to Australia. He had money saved and wanted to start a new life in a new country. This he did soon after and I lost contact.

The next time I heard about John was some years later when I learned of his having returned from Australia with a broken leg and was told that he was a resident at St Lawrence Dene nursing home. John was then only in his early 30s and had been back on the Isle of Wight for six months. Surely his leg had healed well enough for him to return to his relatives and why would he have been placed in a residential nursing home for elderly people? With these questions puzzling me I decided to pay him a visit.

It appeared that, due to his lack of education, he had only managed to pick up casual labour and gardening jobs in Australia and when the money ran out, decided to return to the Island. Just prior to his return he had fallen and broken his leg in two places and had landed with his leg in plaster. All but one of his relatives had since either moved or died

and he found himself, leg heavily plastered, with very little money and nowhere to go. The Social Services decided that a flat was out of the question as there was no way that he could cope on his own. The local hospital was unable to offer him a bed as his leg was healing well and he was able to get around, so the Council, after consultation with their Social Services department, offered him a room at St Lawrence Dene until more permanent and suitable accommodation could be found, in return for which and because of his age, he would assist in the garden.

John was happy with the situation and all went well for a few weeks until one day on returning to his room he found wet muddy footprints on his carpet and damp earth in one corner, as if some one had accidentally knocked over a pot plant. Puzzling over the situation John realised that something was wrong. Firstly, he would not have any cut flowers or pot plants in his room as he was adamant on them being in their place and growing outside. Secondly, he was always careful to lock his door. Working on the land with a load of bush whacking Australian farm labourers had taught him that.

He told me: "I thought maybe some cleaning lady or one of the staff had been in here and had spilt some other persons plant. I thought probably they would have been back to clear it all up but they didn't. So in the end I cleared it up myself."

John then went on to tell me that he

St Lawrence Dene, now the family home of Mr and Mrs R.Linnington.

was woken at about two o'clock that morning by noises which sounded as if a person was walking up and down the corridor outside his room. He quickly got up and opened his door just in time to see an elderly lady in a black coat, with a scarf tied round her neat white hair and wearing brown boots reach the landing and disappear down the stairs towards the rear door.

"I thought it was funny 'cause you can't get anywhere that way except into the garden. Well, who would want to go into the garden at two o'clock in the mornin'?" he asked.

John soon forgot about the incident and continued his gardening. By this time a few weeks had elapsed and the garden was beginning to look completely different under his natural ability and expertise. In fact John was thrilled when one of the residents came up to him, smiled and gestured her appreciation of his work before returning and sitting on the garden seat from where she had been observing him for the past half hour.

It was then that John recognised her as the lady who had disturbed him with her nocturnal wanderings into the garden a few weeks before. She was wearing the same scarf tied round the same neat hair, the same coat and boots. "Was it you I saw goin' into the garden the other night – about two in the mornin'?" asked John, standing up and looking at the garden seat on which was sitting – no one.

Thinking that he had been to engrossed to notice the old lady go in to lunch, John decided that it was about time he made himself ready to do the same. On reaching his room, he once again found the door ajar and upon entering noticed on his table a large flower pot in which was a huge healthy crimson azalea. Where had it come from? John knew all the plants in the garden at St Lawrence Dene and no-where were there any azaleas growing at that time. The pot which contained the plant was standing on some brown paper, on the edge of which were just written two words: 'Thank You'.

John, even more puzzled and making sure that he locked his door, took himself to the dining room and enjoyed lunch, after which he decided to mention the happenings to the duty nurse. Interested much more in seeing the beautiful azalea than attending to what she considered might be John's imaginative stories, she accompanied him upstairs. This time his door had remained securely locked. He opened it, invited the nurse to step inside only to discover that no pot plant was evident, neither was there any sign that it ever had been. Neither was there any brown paper with writing on the edge

Sensing his distress matron immediately knew something was wrong. John was a down-to-earth person who might become a little muddled at times, but would not be able to lie to save his life, neither was he capable of making up this sort of story. After careful questioning and learning about the elderly lady, she knew that something had happened, something quite unusual which within her working knowledge at the Dene had never before occurred.

The lady was perhaps the ghost of a resident who had died five years earlier. She, like John, was always tending the garden and would become rather angry if anyone other than the official gardener touched it.

Nothing ever happened after that and John spent many happy months as a resident and unofficial gardener at St Lawrence Dene. He died in Newport in 1982. The duty nurse and myself both endeavoured to explain the unusual spectre and the events which happened to John but were unable to offer rationality. Was it that the old lady was annoyed at someone taking her place and touching the garden, that the dirt and footsteps were placed in the room and found by John. And then, seeing how excellent he was and how much he loved the garden, forgave him and presented him with the azalea?

How was John's door opened when he was always so careful to lock it after him? Knowing John as I did, he did not have the ability to make up stories of this sort, so how was he able to describe the elderly lady and what she was wearing so accurately . Maybe he knows the answer himself by now. We certainly do not.

Children at the Pottery

IT MAY be thought that Brading, to which we have already been introduced in the story of Louis de Rochfort, would be one of the small Island towns where anyone interested in the supernatural would make their first stop. But, although it is the home of many Bronze Age finds, a third-century Roman villa and centuries ago, a thriving trading post for the Phoenicians, the Kyng's Towne of Brading known as the capital of East Wight until the end of the 18th century, seems to be a little lacking in spectral reports.

I would be most surprised if, over many centuries, there had not been numerous stories of the supernatural but it could be that such reports have been lost in the annals of time, or that they have been added to so much and by now have become so outlandish that their credibility (apart from being amusing stories for a winter night) is non-existent.

However, at the end of the High Street, not far from Graham Osborne-Smith's Wax Museum where lie the remains of Louis de Rochfort, and near the old Town Hall with its miserably small single cell in which miscreants were once locked, and its gruesome display of the town's original mediaeval public whipping post and stocks, there stands yet one more old coach house which is the site of the other credible ghostly occurrence documented in this area. Whether this haunting has any connection with the wax museum we do not know as no historically written accounts are on record.

This old coaching house was, until quite recently, owned by Krystyna Young, who, prior to her purchase sought and obtained the necessary planning permission to convert the downstairs rooms into a pottery and retail outlet. The conversion of the coach house to a pottery was not a long process. As she said "The whole place seemed to lend itself to such activity". Such was her expertise that after the necessary permission had been granted and the details were in order, it did not take too long for her move in and build up an extremely successful business.

Krystyna was a little unusual. She was primarily an artist and like most of her ilk spent much of her time in a world of imaginative thought, designing new patterns and items of pottery which were not only popular but seemed never ending. There, however, the imagination would cease and the practicality would take over. She was regarded and respected as a most astute and strict businesswoman. In fact, Krystyna was probably one of the last people who would wish to speak about the paranormal, yet she was quite unashamed to report her experiences. The noises commenced on the day before the pottery was ready to open to the public. Krystyna described how she had been satisfying herself about last minute details of the layout of the retail part of the premises in the afternoon when she heard noises which she described as children's voices accompanied by footsteps which seemed to be emanating from one of the upstairs rooms. She said that the voices and footsteps were as if children were playing. "The sounds were light and gentle and not in the least frightening. It happened at about three o'clock when children of a bygone age would probably be having their tea with their nanny in the nursery." For many weeks and months the ghostly sounds presumably made by these children would filter downstairs and into the shop. Although with no precise regularity they would occur about two or three times a week and always at the same hour in the afternoon. Krystyna not only began to expect, but even to welcome then. Many times she had gone to examine the first floor bedroom from which the noises seemed to be coming, but was always surprised because they were not getting any louder, even as she climbed the stairs and neared the room, and as soon as she opened the door, they stopped.

The authenticity of this story has never really been doubted as the sounds of the children were noticed and remarked upon by customers who would be in the shop or looking round the pottery when they happened. They would remark to Krystyna about her 'happy children' but she refused to become involved in lengthy explanations or replies.

After a few months, the pottery became so busy that Kyrstyna decided to take on two staff. Not only would she teach them the art of creating a design and throwing and kilning a piece of pottery, but she also trained them to look after the retail side of the business while she was physically producing the ever growing number of articles being purchased by a discerning public.

After extensive interviews, Krystyna decided that two young ladies, one from Brading and the other from nearby St Helen's, fitted the bill.

Krystyna felt duty bound to explain the ghost children to the two girls. Afterwards she said that it was fortunate she had the foresight to do this as the sounds were heard by them on their first afternoon. From then their regularity became almost daily and the two girls, neither of them frightened, were themselves quite disappointed if a day went by without them being heard.

Everything was normal with business improving all the time until the summer of the second year when Krystyna invited some friends to stay. By this time the two young ladies were quite able to handle the pottery, one quite a natural in

The Red Lion, Brading, once Krystyna Young's Pottery. The building was a pub until 1942 and again in the 1990s.

being freezing cold in the night when they were both woken by sounds they described as quarrelling children.

They were reluctant to admit they were scared, as boys of this age often are, and the family put it down to the excitement of the holiday, and thought that the fact they were in strange beds in a strange house may not have been conducive to them sleeping well during the first night. They were told not to worry Krystyna by telling her about this.

The second morning the boys arrived to breakfast obviously terrified, so much so that they refused to spend another night in the room. Apparently the same thing had happened, but this time the children manifested themselves as shadows, running around the room and shouting at each other. Even when the bravest of the lads switched on the light, the sounds did not cease. The room once again became freezing and the terrified boys decided to make a run for it. They both jumped out of bed and went to the door which was somehow jammed or even locked. Eventually both the noises and coldness ceased and the night passed without further incident but neither of them slept.

Why these previously friendly little spirits should suddenly take on the role of instilling fear into the household was

the art of manufacturing and the other equally so in the administration of the business. Krystyna had not enjoyed a break from work since she had moved to the house and she looked forward to a few days out and about with her friends. Alas, this was not to be. It seemed that the spectral children were either more mischievous than at first suspected, or even a more plausible answer, viciously jealous.

The friends arrived, a family with two ten-year-old children who were both allocated to the bedroom whence came the sounds. The first morning when they arrived down for breakfast they seemed a little subdued, completely unlike two healthy young lads who were usually full of excitement at the thought of new adventures, especially in a new place and near the sea.

Finally and after much parental questioning, they spoke of the bedroom never explained. We do know that the visitors did not stay in the house with Krystyna but moved to a nearby hostelry and that not long afterwards Krystyna sold the house and pottery.

The new owners found, to their dismay that they had also bought the ghosts for they too reported many daytime phenomena of childlike footsteps. But now, in addition, from the small room where the little boys who stayed with the Youngs had become so frightened, there were emanating other inexplicable sounds, including the opening and closing of doors during the night. When they went to investigate, though the room felt cold, no other physical signs were apparent. Eventually, it is said, the house was exorcised by a priest and to my knowledge nothing has been reported since.

Although I made extensive enquiries, not only into the history of the property, but where possible about those families who have resided there, I have been unable to unearth any explanation to this phenomena.

What was the reason for the apparently friendly ghost children suddenly acting like nasty little spoilt brats? Was it that other children were staying in what they regarded as their room? Or was it that other children were enjoying, albeit only for a couple of weeks, the affections of Krystyna, a lady who they may have regarded as their property? Who can tell?

The Bard of Farringford

BEDBURY Lane, Freshwater, runs from Freshwater Bay at the east of the village to Alum Bay and the Needles in the west. It is an attractive road winding through glades, pine ridges and the beautiful countryside of the area of the Island known as the West Wight. Travelling in a westerly direction, behind a few large houses on the left is the commencement of the spine of the Isle of Wight called Highdown. One of the largest of these houses, now a luxury hotel, is Farringford House which up to 1892 was the home of Poet Laureate, Alfred Lord Tennyson.

Maybe it is only to be expected that

Farringford House, Freshwater Bay, Isle of Wight.

A likeness of Alfred, Lord Tennyson at Farringford House as displayed at the Isle of Wight Wax Museum, Brading.

the people of Freshwater, Totland and Yarmouth, who tend to regard Tennyson as one of their heroes, formed a Tennyson Society earlier in the 1900s and the Highdown has been unofficially named Tennyson Down.

The down reaches its highest point just prior to the descent to Alum Bay and The Needles and here, both as a navigational beacon and a monument to the great poet, is an obelisk, aptly named Tennyson Monument. Lord Tennyson, who chose as his baronetcy title 1st Baron of Aldworth and Freshwater, was

created Poet Laureate and succeeded William Wordsworth in 1850, altogether a good year as he found fame with his poem *In Memoriam* and married Emily Sellwood. Three years later he moved to the Island after entering into an agreement with the Seymours, who owned Farringford House, to rent it furnished for £2 per week on a three-year lease with an option to buy, which he eventually did. On first seeing the house he described it as being 'like blank verse which suited the humblest cottage and the grandest cathedral'. He also owned

The grave of Emily, Lady Tennyson, wife of Alfred, Lord Tennyson, in All Saints' Parish Churchyard, Freshwater.

another house in Aldworth, Sussex, hence his title, but in his latter years, hardly ever left the Island, being flattered by the patronage of Her Majesty, Queen Victoria and her husband, Prince Albert, the Prince Regent, both of whom then resided for most of the year at Osborne House in East Cowes. In fact Prince Albert became quite a friend of Tennyson and a frequent visitor to Farringford House. Why Tennyson ever chose to live on the Island, apart from being near to the seat of Victoriana which he loved so much, we will never know. He was known to have detested the sea. Maybe this was one of the reasons he chose to stay in Freshwater. Apart from a few official trips abroad he would often visit Ireland which he dearly loved and did not consider 'abroad' in the true sense of the word. Visits to foreign countries he would always enjoy, but he hated the

preparation and was always ready to come home to Freshwater, invariably dropping off at Aldworth on the way. As he became older his travels became less, even to his beloved Galway.

Lord Tennyson adored walking over Highdown, invariably dressed in his green top coat and a wide brimmed hat. He became a great favourite with the locals who adopted him as 'their friend and poet' and would always stop and pass the time of day. Sometimes his servants would rush from the house and inform him that HRH Prince Albert was awaiting him in his library, whereupon Tennyson would return and entertain the prince for hours.

In 1892, after a long period of suffering caused mainly by gout and rheumatism, Alfred Lord Tennyson, much loved of poets and a much-loved man on the Isle of Wight, died whilst on a visit to his other home in Aldworth. He was buried with full ceremony at Poets' Corner in Westminster Abbey and a period of deep mourning was observed on the Island, especially in Freshwater.

It was a few months later that reports started to filter through that a man, wearing a green top coat and a wide brimmed hat was often seen walking the Highdown.

This, so soon after Tennyson's death, incensed the good people of West Wight. That a person could impersonate their favourite son and poet was not only in bad taste but morally unforgivable.

A committee was set up in order to do something about this, resulting in some residents forming a group and waiting on the lonely Highdown for this impostor to appear. He never did, at least while they were present, but soon after wards more reports were being circulated about this man being seen by ordinary people at various times during the day and night. Absolutely determined now not to allow this to go on, the residents from Freshwater, Totland and Yarmouth banded together and worked out a watch system. In vain they waited on the cold, misty Highdown until early January 1893 when their patience was rewarded and they spotted the man approaching. He had obviously not seen them hiding in their ambush position.

Suddenly they sprung and challenged the green-robed figure but what happened then filled them with dread. As one of them said later: "It was impossible to understand". As one of the largest of the men tried to apprehend what he thought to be the impostor, the figure walked right through him, then on through many of the others before disappearing into thin air just before reaching the gardens of Farringford House. Asked after the event, the man told a reporter that it was just as if a cold, damp piece of blotting paper had passed through his arm. "Everywhere suddenly turned cold," he said. "I am convinced that what I and so many others saw and had reported was the spirit of Lord Tennyson. You see, I knew him so well"

Another sighting was reported 80 years later in the 1970s. This time Lord Tennyson did not appear but, from what we are able to ascertain, the spirit of Emily, his wife, and one of their sons, Lionel, who died in 1866 whilst on route home from India, together with a third party, all appeared.

In the Parish Church of All Saints', Freshwater there is a plaque in memory to the unfortunate Lionel Tennyson commemorating his demise on that fateful trip, whilst outside in the gravelled churchyard, Emily lies in her stone tomb.

One Saturday evening in the late 1970s, George Morgan, a Highdown sheep farmer, was walking past the Red Lion in Freshwater Old Village and saw three people walking towards the lychgate of the church. To his horror and amazement, instead of opening the gate to enter the churchyard, they seemed to just float through it.

From the description of the people he was able to give, there seems little doubt that he saw Emily, Lady Tennyson and her son, Lionel. The identity of the third person we will never know for certain but it is thought that it was the ghost of the financial advisor to the Kalid of Egypt, whose grave is nearby beneath a large white marble angel.

The Returning Undertaker

AN AUTHOR'S research usually takes many forms, uses many sources and consults many people, all this adding up to many hours, days and sometimes even weeks spent on this part of the work. Some of the sources prove complicated, such as locating the correct person to guide you through historical records locked away in dusty archives. Church registers, monasteries and religious outlets are slightly easier, as, in general, are newspapers and the media mainly because cooperation is nearly always willingly given and forthcoming. Tracking down, making appointments and interviewing people can also be time consuming. A regular part of research, however, comes from books, and apart from the more usual libraries, together with tour guides and pamphlets relating to a given area, ordinary bookstalls provide a researcher with a wealth of information. Patience is essential, but after a while it is easy to develop a 'knack' and adopt a pattern which may help cut down a little of the time.

A simple, interesting and sometimes a most rewarding way of collecting what could be useful information can be car boot or jumble sales where bookstalls are invariably profuse. Much information may be obtainable, not only by meeting and talking to ordinary, decent and interesting people, but for anyone interested in books, as most of us are, many good bargains are often obtainable – even if at the end of the day you find little information of your subject. Myself and my team are trained not to pass these by.

It was as a result of a conversation with one such stallholder at a Red Cross table top sale, that I heard the story of the undertaker who announced his own death to members of his family.

Newport businessman David Grant had recently retired due to having undergone a successful hip replacement operation from which he was recovering. Unfortunately his other hip was also suspect and he had been advised that it, too, should be replaced. David found that manning his stall at various charitable sales not only helped him therapeutically but also allowed him to meet and communicate with different people.

After chatting for a few minutes about my own books and those of other local authors, we managed to latch on to the subject of the paranormal and ghosts in general. He was pleased to relate an experience which occurred to him personally many years before and gave me permission relate it to you in *Web of Fear*.

The story involved his grandfather, who, at the precise time of his death, appeared to both he and his mother. Although David was a young lad on the Isle of Wight at the time, his grandfather's death happened many miles away in Grimsby where he was a local undertaker.

As a boy, David lived with his parents in a house in Lake, a village between Sandown and Shanklin on the eastern coast of the Island. Their home was a typical council house of the period with an old type gas cooker and a deep sink, complete with wooden draining board. David was a typical Isle of Wight lad of the time who would have his chores to complete before going out with his friends.

One Saturday in 1946, David was at home with his mother. They had just had lunch and both had just completed washing up. The weather was rather chilly as it was autumn and the day had started misty. Looking at the sea, David decided that it would be damp, chilly and not the sort of weather to be out with friends for any length of time, so he decided to spend the afternoon indoors.

His mother had gone into the sitting room where the cheerful fire was throwing out a comfortable heat and replenished the fuel by placing some thick logs on a base of coal. Meanwhile David had put away the crockery and made a pot of tea which he took into the lounge and both settled in the comfortable armchairs in front of the open fire.

They had just sat down and were enjoying their tea when they heard a noise at the front door. It was not a knock and whoever it was had certainly not used the loud bell. "It was just a noise but sufficient to make me put down my tea." said David.

He remembered clearly having to place the cat, who had settled on his lap, into the chair as he rose and walked towards the sitting room door which led along the passageway to the front. He remembers his mother saying that she did not think it was really a knock and not to bother, but David, who was already up and not extremely popular with one disturbed puss cat, was already on his way to see what the noise was. There, smiling in greeting and obviously glad to be in the warm after his journey, stood his grandfather. Calling to his mother he said loudly, "Mum, Grandad's here," and within seconds Mrs Grant had joined them in the passage.

Reflecting for a moment David told me. "I had always admired my grandfather who was an undertaker in Grimsby. When I think of him, I remember his black suit. He was a tall, upright man who always wore a full Albert chain attached to his watch which I think was a gold half hunter, something which I admired. I remember, he wore a tall black hat when he walked in front of his horse-drawn hearse, not like the motorcade we have today.

"Happier times, however would see him wearing a trilby and that is exactly how I saw him standing there, just inside the passageway."

Continuing with the story he said: "My mother said, 'Oh, hello Dad, come on in'. My grandfather smiled, just pulled out his watch from his waistcoat pocket, looked at the time and to the amazement of both mother and me, slowly seemed to vaporise before our eyes.

"By now we were both extremely frightened and returned to the sitting room. I remember the time. It was exactly 1.45pm and I distinctly remember mother asking me this, saying she would have to tell my uncle about it and ask him what it meant.

"I was very nervous all the evening and to be honest, a little afraid that something was wrong, but didn't know just how wrong until the next morning, when we received a telegram.

"My mother was one of a large family and it was her sister who sent the telegram bearing the news that grandfather had passed away at 1.45pm the day before. Mother had always been her father's favourite and I must admit that I seemed to be one of his favourite grandsons," he said.

Was it for this reason that the old undertaker appeared at their house in Lake and was he trying somehow to communicate with them? These are questions the answers to which would be merely pure conjecture and therefore something with which I do not wish to become involved, but since this story was related to me, I have come to know David well and am pleased to report that his second hip replacement operation was as successful as his first.

He is a first-rate business man and a person well thought of in the community – not someone who would be likely to suffer with a 'fermented imagination'. In fact, just the very reverse. Besides, Mrs Grant witnessed the same apparition at the same time.

One more small point on which David often reflects. He said. "At the time the visit from grandad seemed quite natural and it was not until much later that Mother and myself both realised the importance of one fact. He had no door key and the front door was always latched. It was the same that day. How did the old man get in?"

The Mistletoe Bough

LET US now travel a little further afield, leaving the Island for a while. We journey in fact to the outer limits of the beautiful county of Hampshire, to the village of Bramshill and a beautifully kept drive just over one mile long which leads to Bramshill House, now a police college. It is a large Jacobean fronted house with a perfect gabled roof. Could this be the same Bramshill which has known such tragedy and wherein once took place the Legend of the Mistletoe Bough?

The mistletoe hung in the castle hall
The holly branch shone on the old oak wall
And the Baron's retainers were blithe and gay
And keeping their Christmas Holy Day
The Baron beheld with a father's pride
His beautiful child, young Lovell's bride.

These words were immortalised by Haymes Bailey in his 1828 poem *The Mistletoe Bough* and tell the story of a marriage which took place in the early 18th century and the untimely death of the bride.

Bramshill, or Bromeselle as it was first known in Saxon times, can be traced back to the days of Edward the Confessor. There is a mention of Bromeselle in the Domesday book. Its owner, Hugh de Port, is also registered and described as 'a Leviathan of Hampshire Landowners'. The De Port family were to retain ownership for a further nine generations before the house was passed to St John of Basing and subsequently to Sir John Foxley.

It is the Foxley family we have to thank for the first house on this site, for Sir John was the Constable of Windsor Castle and in charge of reconstruction work. Many of Bramshill's designs reflect those of the Castle. He also built a chapel, enclosed thousands of acres of land which was laid down as deer parks and built the house on the hill of Broom.

The present house was the work of Edward, Lord Zouche of Harringwoth, who in 1605 demolished the greater part of the old residence and started to build it as we know it today. Much of the material of the old building was incorporated into the new, which, when completed in 1612, was a most majestic place with many vast rooms. The walls were covered with rare tapestries, and the long gallery was twice the length of a cricket pitch.

On completion it was to be a gift to Henry, Prince of Wales, eldest son of James I, but the Prince was to die tragically before it was finished.

It was while Lord Zouche lived in the great house that he invited the Archbishop of Canterbury, The Most Reverent George Abbot, to join him for the hunting season. When stalking some deer, the Archbishop, who was a noted marksman, saw a movement in the undergrowth, took aim and felled what he thought was a lordly stag, only to discover later that he had mistaken a keeper for the beast. The keeper sustained injuries from which he did not recover.

Unable to live with his conscience, George Abbot withdrew from all public engagements intending to resign from his high office, but was persuaded to await the outcome of an ecclesiastical enquiry. After long debate the ecclesiastical court decided that the Archbishop was in no way to blame and asked him to continue his good work. It is reported, however, that he was never to smile again.

In 1699 Bramshill was sold to the Cope Family. On Christmas Eve 1727 with the house bedecked with holly, tragedy struck! Anne, the eldest daughter of the sixth baronet Sir John Cope, was married to Hugh Bethell from Yorkshire. After the wedding breakfast the bride wanted to play a game of hide-and-seek. The bridegroom and the guests were to search everywhere for Anne but alas she was not to be found. Years went by without news. It was only when some of the servant girls went into a long disused part of the house and examined a chest, the lock of which could only be opened from the outside, that they found the body of the poor unfortunate bride Anne, still clutching a small sprig of mistletoe.

Anne Bethell (née Cope) was buried in January 1729. The family were so grief-stricken that they had the whole of the wing of the house in which the tragedy took place demolished.

It was six years before Bailey's poem *The Mistletoe Bough* with its haunting stanza was published. Also during that time an almost identical poem was written by Samuel Rogers, a friend of Lord Byron. Rogers was to place the tragedy in Italy. In the 18th century, Sir John Cope, Anne's father was also was to travel to many parts of Europe. Could Rogers have heard it from Sir John when on his travels and plagiarised the tragic English story?

By the mid-18th century reports began circulating that Anne's ghost had been seen walking in the house, wearing her white wedding gown and still carrying her sprig of mistletoe. The sightings have been many over the years up to and including a visit to Bramshill by the King and Queen of Romania and their family during World War Two. Indeed, at one point Her Majesty asked if the children could be moved as a ghostly lady dressed in white and carrying a sprig of mistletoe had been seen several times during the night in their room.

The mystery has deepened over the years and perhaps it is no more than a legend without foundation, but no one has ever disputed the sightings of Anne, the Lady in White.

Today, when entering the Police College at Bramshill, easily noticeable and standing in the entrance hall is a large chest. There is no doubt in the mind of anyone as to the authenticity of its caption, 'The Mistletoe Bough Chest'.

As if this ghostly apparition were not enough for Bramshill, many other sightings have also been reported.

One of the first commandants of the college was standing with a police officer on the terrace. Looking along the drive they saw an intruder on the little bridge which crossed a stream. The officer went to apprehend him but was quite shaken on arriving at the bridge to find that the stranger had disappeared, in spite of the fact that there was nowhere that he could possibly have taken cover.

This is just one of the many strange happenings which have been documented as having taken place near the stream known as the Pale Pond. Over the years horsemen have told of the difficulty in controlling their mounts which shied when passing this pond.

It was by the side of this water that little Penelope Cope in her pushchair gave both her mother and nanny cause for great consternation when she started talking about a green man. Apparently he would appear not only by the pond, but anywhere near water. She saw him (or so she said) by any puddle, lake, or even near her bath. When asked to describe the figure, the child would reply, "Just like Daddy, but he has no legs."

Mrs Denzil Cope, Penelope's mother, had been assured that there were no ghosts at Bramshill, the stories being mere fiction.

Delving into the family's past she unearthed details of a Cope ancestor who had a passion for the colour green.

In fact, he dressed entirely in green. He wore green gloves and carried a green whip. He would only have green furniture, and the house itself was painted green. He would even live solely on green fruit and vegetables. Only his boots were black. Could this account for the child being unable to see legs?

This ancestor was to 'meet his Maker' in 1806 when it is believed he threw himself from high cliffs into the sea. Later, Mrs Denzil Cope was to see an apparition herself, for, waking one morning she was visited by the Bramshill Grey Lady. She saw a beautiful woman with lovely golden hair by her bed. The ghost was in a shroud like a grey dress and was accompanied by an overpowering scent of lilies. The figure and aroma were to appear several times to both Mrs Cope and her children, each time in their different bedrooms. The children's description of the figure was identical to that seen by their mother with the exception that she appeared to the children within an aura of soft light. They said that she looked sad and they could often see tear drops on her cheeks. Sometimes her hair would be untidy as if she had just risen from her bed and she would often point to the window, wearing that grey sleeveless robe.

Yet another spectre seen at Bramshill often manifests itself in the long gallery at about midnight when one is able to detect the aroma of perfume, followed by the sight of the figure of a beautiful young woman dressed in flowing white, running through the lonely corridors and sometimes out into the garden. Penelope's great grandfather, Sir William Cope together with members of his family were on the terrace one evening. Seeing a white robed figure at the far end leaning over the balustrade, Sir William sent one of his staff to investigate. At first the member of staff was unable to see the person but as he advanced along the terrace he perceived the figure leap over the balustrade and disappear. No explanation has ever been found to answer this strange apparition, but certainly all present attested to the sight.

It has long been said that Bramshill is the most haunted house in Hampshire and the more I have researched into this, the more I have come to believe it. Sightings of apparitions have been collaborated by many people. Three of the most frequent of these seem to occur when walking the passageways where often people experience a strong sense of foreboding, and ghostly figures have been seen in the Fleur de Lys room. There is also the ghost of a little old man with a flowing beard who peers through the hall windows and many have described the chapel drawing room as often being crowded 'with people from another age'. It is reputed that a guest staying at Bramshill, on entering her room felt the hand of a small child thrust into her own. Although there was no feeling of fear, whilst the little hand held hers she was overcome with grief.

Most people who have seen the apparitions make the same remark which is that the ghostly figures seem to float about two feet off the ground. We know that at one time, prior to structural alterations, the floors had been much higher. Could it be that these spirits are walking on the original floors? Among the many having seen these phenomena are included civilian staff, a Red Cross worker and some builders. In 1962, Fred Cook, an employee at Bramshill, who has spent nearly 40 years working within the walls of this mansion of mystique, related some of his experiences. He stated that from time to time, various people would tell him of an encounter with the Grey Lady. He invariably explained it away by saying that it was a trick of moonlight and would reassure everyone that were no such things as ghosts. He said that it was hard enough to keep staff at Bramshill without encouraging rumours.

One day a member of staff told Fred that a lady in a grey costume had walked through his bedroom late at night. He was assured that there were no ghosts, but returned the following day and stated categorically that, once again, this Grey Lady had visited him in his bedroom. Being a man of the world, and having been told that it was no ghost, he jumped out of bed and tried to grab her round the waist, but she just dissolved in his arms, leaving behind a strong aroma of lilies.

It was, in fact, Fred Cook who was summoned to deal with the King and Queen of Romania and their family whom we mentioned earlier.

When, Fred, a self-confessed sceptic, was finally to meet the apparition of the Grey Lady for himself, his actions spoke louder than any previous words. Late one evening he was making his customary tour of the house before locking up, accompanied by his big labrador dog. As he opened the door of the long gallery, standing there staring at him, was the Grey Lady. If Fred were mistaken, then his dog certainly was not. Giving a howl of terror she ran from the house in the direction of home as fast as her four legs would carry her with poor Fred only just behind. After arriving home, although still shaken he remembered his responsibilities and, taking what courage he had left, made his way back to the long gallery, minus the shivering dog who had no intention of leaving the fireside again that night. Opening the big door and cautiously peering in, he found it to be completely empty. Only the scent of lilies remained.

After completing his rounds he made his way out of Bramshill and down the long drive towards his own house. As he did so, Fred Cook had the distinct feeling he was being followed by someone or something which seemed to be getting nearer and nearer all the time. Whatever was there left him as he went through the manor gates. He made sure that he never walked along that part of the drive again, except in daylight.

He tried to explain all this to the lady who owned the cottage in which he was staying at the time and she replied that he was not the only one to report experiencing this terror. She told him that she, herself, was walking her dogs in the same place one evening at dusk when she felt a sense of panic. Her dogs seemed to cringe with fear, then howling, they raced away. She assured Fred that she, too, would never walk along there again.

As Peter Underwood stated in his book *Ghosts of Hampshire and the Isle of Wight*: 'Not without cause has Bramshill been described as the most haunted house in Hampshire.'

Squire Bathurst of Itchell Manor

IN 1643, Parliamentarian forces, commonly called the Roundheads, prepared to do battle with the Royalists at Crondall. The Roundheads under their leader Sir William Waller took up their positions at Crondall Church. The use of a churchyard as a fortification was a common practice of the day with the Parliamentary armies and at this battle Sir William was to rout the Royalists, driving them back as far as Oxford and Newbury, but unfortunately with great loss of life on both sides. The parish church of All Saints', Crondall still bears many scars of the ferocity of the fighting and it is small wonder that there are many ghostly sightings of Sir William's mounted troopers, riding along the avenue of lime trees and entering the churchyard.

But this is but one small and probably the best known report attributed to this area. The main story is that of a large manor house nearby.

The 15th century Itchell Manor was destroyed by fire in 1680 and was to remain a ruin until 1701. In 1800 it became the home of the Lefroy family and during that time many apparitions and manifestations were reported, not only by them, but also by their guests and staff. Phantom coaches and horses would be heard driving up to the manor.

One such sound was heard and reported by a new tutor who was at the time sitting in the morning room writing. It was late in the evening and dark outside as he rose from his table to look out of the window which overlooked the drive. Maybe he was inquisitive as to who would call at such an hour. Baffled when finding the drive completely empty, he became more than a little frightened, so much so that he immediately extinguished the light and proceeded upstairs with the intention of retiring. Such was his mental state that he was unable to locate his room. He wandered the passageways and corridors of the house in dismay for what seemed to him like hours until eventually he was found in an extremely distraught condition by his host. From that day the tutor would insist on being escorted to his room every night.

It is said that before the Lefroys came to the manor, the then owner Squire Bathurst was set upon by a highwayman when travelling on Bagshot Heath. Both the squire and postillion were killed, and since then a coach and horse were often heard arriving back at the house. Another story states that Squire Bathurst, having been surprised by his valet

Crondell Village, scene of some of the fiercest fighting in the English Civil War.

when counting his money, lost his temper and murdered him, then fearful of reprisal bricked the valet up in the wall of the bedroom called the Little Highlander. Afterwards, banging on the panelling would often be heard.

One evening Charles Lefroy was sitting late into the night writing when he heard footsteps approaching the bedroom door. Then hearing a cry thought it was one of the children who was unable to sleep. He opened the door only to find that the long passageway was deserted. Then, hurrying to the children's room, he found them all fast asleep. Next morning the nurse confirmed that the children had slept soundly all night, but that she too had heard the footsteps and a child's cry.

Throughout the period that the Lefroy family owned the manor they found difficulty in keeping servants. The main complaint was of the ghostly noises which would haunt the house starting at about 11 o'clock at night and continuing until well into the early hours. On two occasions Mrs Elizabeth Lefroy, by then an elderly lady, was reading family prayers when they were interrupted by these footsteps.

The 16th-century brick tower of All Saints' Church, Crondall.

17th century. These strange phenomena were to continue, even after part of the old wing was pulled down and rebuilt

From many accounts recorded over the centuries, there is little doubt that Itchell Manor was subject to many strange and noisy happenings until its final demolition in 1954.

On a summer's day when travelling through the green lanes in this pleasant corner of Hampshire, it is hard to think of haunted manors and the like, but in this serene setting encompassing the villages from Bramshott to Buriton it is said that you are in the most haunted part of Hampshire.

Here will be found old manor houses nestling among the fields, small brooks babbling through lush and quiet meadows and old churches, complete with yew trees. It was also the home of the king of horror movies, the late Boris Karloff, who at one time was asked by well-known author Peter Underwood and reported in his book *Ghosts of Hampshire and the Isle of Wight* if he had ever experienced any ghosts or apparitions. "No!" he replied, and added "But from my experience of human beings, when they see me in the flesh, the ghosts would probably be so scared that they would disappear before I did."

During renovations an old painting of Squire Bathurst was found behind some panelling in the Little Highlander bedroom. There are a number of authenticated accounts of Itchell Manor being haunted by ghostly noises even in the

Death and Debauchery

ON AN area of land adjacent to Portsmouth Dockyard there once stood an impressive inn, the name of which was indelibly written on the heart of many a naval officer who served at the time of sailing ships. As to the name of this hostelry, my research has produced two, the Blue Posts and the Admiral Collingwood. Further research has led me to believe that there was a Blue Posts Inn situated in Broad Street, which was the particular haunt of midshipmen during the Napoleonic wars. Therefore it is my intention for the sake of the report of this apparition to use the name the Blue Posts.

Of the Blue Posts there is a fascinating story which is to be found in the diaries of the Revd Richard Harris Barham and claims to be one of the most authenticated ghost stories in existence.

It was towards the end of the 18th century when a certain Mr Hamilton arrived at Portsmouth. The same day several naval ships had also docked and many of their discharged crews were roaming the streets in a drunken state.

Having no wish to become involved in the drunkenness and debauchery that was so evident around him, Hamilton took a room at the Blue Posts and after doing full justice to a large meal decided to retire for the night, informing the landlady that he had no wish to be disturbed. He was then told by his hostess that only a twin-bedded room was available and, as was the custom in those days, he would have to share.

Remembering the scenes of debauchery he had no wish to do so and offered to pay his hostess for both beds on the understanding that no matter what happened, his privacy would be respected and maintained, and that no one would be allowed to use the second bed. This was agreed, so having paid he made his way upstairs to his room overlooking Broad Street. By the light of his candle he read his Bible for approximately half an hour, then checking to ascertain that the door was secured from the inside, he extinguished the flame and was soon asleep. During the night he was woken by the sound of a general commotion outside. Going over to the window and looking down into Broad Street he could see a group of sailors arguing with the landlady, and as he returned to his bed he was surprised to see that, in spite of his instructions to the contrary, the second bed was occupied by a sleeping man.

Anger welled up within him when he realised that the agreement made earlier had apparently been broken, but just having heard the commotion downstairs he decided to leave reprimanding the landlady until the morning.

The next thing to awaken Hamilton was sunshine streaming in through the window and his first thoughts were of the other man in the second bed still sleeping. By now fully awake in the sunlit room he could see that this man appeared to be a sailor as he was wearing clothes typical of those following the sea as a profession. His most distinctive feature was a large, bushy, black beard which covered most of his face. What perturbed Hamilton most, however, was that he wore a white headscarf in the manner of a seaman which was saturated in blood. Now, not only annoyed about his lack of privacy, Hamilton became a little afraid when he remembered that he had locked and bolted the door from the inside. Quickly checking he was amazed to find the bolts still in place, the door locked and the key still within.

Deciding that he must quiz this man as to his method of entry, he turned to face the bed. To his utter amazement, the bed was empty, but on the pillow was the indentation of the man's head and still visible were his bloodstains.

By now more than just a little perturbed, he quickly dressed and made his way downstairs to confront the landlady who vehemently denied all knowledge of a second person being allowed into the room, saying that she was an honest person and it would have

been most unfair on her part to allow another guest to share. As evidence, she reminded Hamilton that by his own words the door was locked, bolted, and the key turned from the inside and assured him that there was no hidden second entrance.

Still not satisfied, Hamilton went on to describe the man, emphasising not only the bloodstained headscarf, but also his black, bushy whiskers. It was then that the landlady grabbed the bar for support and cried out in a loud voice, "Lord, have mercy upon me!"

Hamilton, by now extremely worried, noticed that the landlady had taken on an extremely pallid complexion and looked as if she was ready to pass on to the next world. Helping her to the nearest chair, Hamilton listened while she began to offer the only possible explanation.

Two nights earlier there had been a party of drunken sailors at the inn and as so often happened when they first came ashore, many fights would ensue, usually over girls of ill repute who 'plied their trade' among the home-coming sailors. During one such argument, in spite of her attempts to intervene, drinking pots, chairs and tables were all upturned and thrown around. A party of marines sitting at one of the tables joined in the mêlée and during the ensuing fracas one of them felled a bewhiskered matelot. It was obvious that he was badly injured, for blood was pouring from the wound and attempts to staunch the flow with a white headscarf

Portsmouth Dockyard gate.

proved completely useless. Offering to give what help she could, the hostess gave instructions for him to be carried into the room which Hamilton had rented. It was however, to no avail, for he died a few hours later.

Both the marines and the matelots knew that many of them would end up hanging from the yardarm if the news of the murder got out so they persuaded the landlady to bury the body in the back garden of the inn. At first she refused, knowing the dire consequences to herself should the matter ever become known to the authorities, but as the amount of money offered as a bribe increased, so her will crumbled until, at last, she agreed and it was decided that the body would be buried in the garden. Now as she turned her eyes to the Heavens above she called for forgiveness in her part of this denial of a decent resting place, for she was to say to Hamilton, "The money has all been in vain. The restless spirit of this poor murdered seaman has come back to take his revenge on me."

Remaining with the Royal Navy, but leaving the age of sail we turn to a more recent account of ghostly apparitions, this time occurring approximately 16 miles north of the city of Portsmouth on the outskirts of Petersfield at the now redundant shore station HMS *Mercury*. This naval training establishment was home to 60 officers and 500 ratings at any one time, who were undergoing training in preparation for a communications career in the 'Silent Service'.

In the mid-1960s it was decided to add further buildings to the old establishment of *Mercury*. The new building was to be called Eagle Block and as was the vogue at that time it took on the appearance of a gigantic block of concrete, something akin to a dockside warehouse. Although lacking in both character and style, it had one thing that many of the older buildings did not – a ghost.

One raw wintery day in February 1961, with Eagle Block well under construction, a piece of plate glass fell from the half finished walls and struck a young rating serving in the WRNS whilst she was going about her normal duty. She was immediately taken to the sick bay but the medical staff could see that she was seriously injured and she was rushed to hospital. In spite of all the efforts of the hospital staff, it was to no avail and she died soon after admission. After the usual inquiries, work continued on Eagle Block.

As training got under way in the new building, complaints were soon being lodged by officers and ratings alike that despite being fed by the same heating system as the other older buildings, Eagle Block was always considerably

colder than the rest. Soon an apparition of a young woman's face apparently trapped in one of the upper rooms was reported. These reports were to come in thick and fast and at first they were not taken seriously. Finally, however, an investigation of the room where the apparition was stated to have been seen was instigated, but each time it proved to be, although unlocked, always empty.

It was not until Saturday, 10 July 1976 that evidence of something 'not being quite right' was officially accepted, and here I quote from the Royal Navy *Communicator* magazine which recorded the occurrence.

"On the night, at 21.50, the foot patrol reported a light on in Eagle Block – 26 classroom – despite the fact that rounds had been going on all day and nobody had seen it previously. At 21.52 the patrol entered the block and reported hearing noises upstairs. At 22.00, the leading hand of the emergency party went to assist and at 22.05, the Firefly was called out to illuminate the roof. The Petty Officer of the Guard found the roof door open and it was assumed that an intruder had broken into the block. At 22.07 a light came on in the Wrens' heads, and the Firefly driver reported possible movements upstairs in the block. At 22.28, after a complete search of the block had drawn a blank, the block was secured. The light in classroom 26 was left in the 'on' position as the 'pull cord' had broken when the patrol had tried to switch it off. At 23.33, the patrol reported the light had mysteriously switched itself off". It is the only reported incident that I have been able to find which has the backing of a naval patrol as a witness.

Now I hope the reader will forgive me if I digress a little beyond the boundaries of Hampshire.

One would think that with a ship as famous as HMS *Victory* lying within its dockyard that there must have been at least one sighting of one of the thousands of seamen who have passed over her decks. After all, at the Battle of Trafalgar, not only was Nelson killed but so too were 57 other gallant seamen. One may be forgiven for presuming that there would be at least one discontented spirit lurking within the area of the dockyard.

I would like to take you back in time to the year 1759 and east to the naval dockyard at Chatham in Kent, where Prime Minister Pitt laid down orders for the building of *Victory*. She was to be so named because of the years of victories for the British armed forces.

In 1770, there came to the dockyard a young boy wishing to go to sea and it was to the *Raisonnable* under the command of Maurice Suckling, his uncle, that he reported and was taken on as a midshipman. His name, Horatio Nelson.

I think therefore, that I can be forgiven for saying that the spiritual home of the world's most famous admiral must be Chatham.

The vision most people have of Admiral Nelson is that of an upright, visually handicapped (having lost the sight of his right eye at the siege of Calvi) and one armed man (having lost his right arm during the attempted seizure of the Spanish treasure ship *Santa Cruz*). Nelson, it has been claimed, does in fact walk the ancient pathways of Chatham's Royal Dockyard, but this apparition is that of the young lad.

Those responsible for the security of the buildings and ropehouse have, on occasions, witnessed this form of a young boy who appears to be dressed in clothes of an earlier age and who, when approached, disappears.

I feel that perhaps there is too much being read into the apparition attributed to be Nelson, for in the 1780s the building was used for the spinning and laying of rope needed for the rigging of warships and it was common place for young boys to be employed. According to a report dated 1810, some of these boys were as young as eight years and fatal accidents were not unknown.

Before returning to Hampshire, I would like to quote the famous diarist Samuel Pepys. His entry on 8 April 1661: '8th. Then to Hill-House at Chatham, where I never was before, and I found a pretty pleasant house, and am pleased with the arms that hang up there. Here we supped very merry, and late to bed; Sir William telling me that old Edgeborrow, his predecessor, did die and walk in my chamber, did make me somewhat afraid, but not so much as, for mirth sake, I did seem. So to bed in the treasurer's chamber.

'9th. Lay and slept well 'till three in

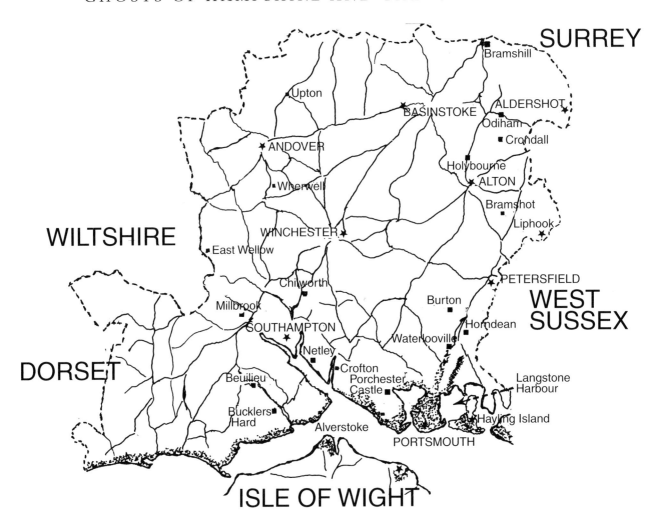

the morning, and then waking, and by the light of the moon I saw my pillow (which overnight I flung from me) stand upright; but not bethinking myself what it might be, I was a little afraid, but sleep overcame all, and so lay till nigh morning, at which time I had a candle brought me, and a good fire made, and in general it was a great pleasure all the time I stayed here..."

So even in those far off days of yesteryear, apparitions were not above visiting the extremely notable diarist Samuel Pepys.

The Contented Ghost of Beaulieu

SOME years before King John signed the Magna Carta in 1215 he had a dream. It could probably be regarded more as a 'nightmare', during which a group of people somehow managed to gain entrance to where he was staying, dragged him off, tried and convicted him and sentenced him to be flogged. The charge was that he had offended both the people and the Church.

He was taken to a public place, stripped of all clothing, tied to a whipping post and beaten so mercilessly, that within his dream he was aware that he must have committed grievous sins and indiscretions although he was equally unaware just what form these could have taken.

He woke next morning in a sweat of terror and found that there were livid marks across his body. He called his chaplains who were quick witted enough to make the most of this Royal Repentance and reminded the King that he had been an enemy of the Church, forcing the Cistercians out of their monastery in Berkshire under pain of their abbots being trampled to death and that this, surely, must be God's punishment for such an ignoble deed.

The dream must have been extremely vivid for King John to listen to his chaplains, and this normally fickle monarch was never to deviate from this act of expiation. In seeking to make his peace with God, the king released a group of Cistercian monks whom he had previously imprisoned, hoping that this action would appease the people.

He then set about performing what some say was his only worthy deed, laying the foundations of the Abbey Church at Beaulieu. As time went on he became so interested in the project that he was to visit many times to watch the work in progress and made it known that he wished to be buried under the high altar. This was not to be, but Ysabella, the King's daughter-in-law, when on her death bed asked if she could be interred at the Abbey. This wish was granted and she was entombed before the altar in the year 1230.

The Abbey was dedicated in the presence of John's son, Henry III, and enjoyed Royal favour until the disillusion in 1536. Edward III bestowed the right of sanctuary and a tun of wine annually and it is recorded that two illustrious persons were to make use of this sanctuary; Margaret of Anjou (the 'She-wolf of France') during the Wars of the Roses,

Beaulieu, the former outer gatehouse with a 19th-century clock turret.

Beaulieu Parish Church showing the view through the Chapter Houses arches to the cloister and the former refectory, now the parish church of the Blessed Virgin and Child.

and the Countess of Warwick (wife of the King Maker) who sought sanctuary there on the eve of the fateful Battle of Barnet and was to remain there for 14 years. It was on the Dissolution that the abbey and all its lands were sold for the sum of £1,350 to Thomas Wrothesley, later to become Earl of Southampton. The sudden end to centuries-old traditions of work and worship of the monks must have been a calamity which is hard for us to imagine today. In retrospect it is easy to understand why their departed spirits retained contact with the place which they had so venerated.

Beaulieu is a small, historic village snuggled peacefully in one of the most beautiful parts of south Hampshire, and it was there I was invited to meet the present owner, Lord Montagu, and archivist Sue Tomkins.

Reports of various apparitions, mostly monks who walk in the cloisters, the aroma of incense, unexplained lights and the singing of a choir late at night, have been passed down from father to son since the middle of the 16th century. Even during the day ghosts can be seen with great clarity. It appears, however, that all the spectres blend in with the

Beaulieu, the Parish House.

quiet and peaceful atmosphere of the ruined Abbey. Lord Montagu himself has said that, of their existence there can be no doubt. Beaulieu is a world famous tourist attraction and many hundreds of thousands of visitors pass through each year and it is impossible to discount the numerous reports from so many different people at different times.

"None of our ghosts have ever been anything but extremely friendly," he said.

Unfortunately it has been virtually impossible to obtain anything but fragmented – and therefore unreliable – information about the spectres at Beaulieu Abbey prior to the early 1900s. We know that there were reports of noises and furniture being moved, doors slamming and footsteps, both climbing the stairs and in the rooms and corridors. These would be heard quite often but no explanation has ever been forthcoming.

Staff and visitors alike have often reported seeing the ghost of a single monk wandering around the Abbey and grounds. In 1927 a member of staff who lived in a room within the Abbey grounds said that she often saw a lone monk and at times heard his footsteps and the sound of his keys being rattled as if he were calling the other monks

The main village street over which the swans flew at the time of the birth of the present Lord Montagu.

who once lived there to matins. When two friends were staying with her and she told them the story of her friendly monk, they laughed it off – that was until one evening at dinner when the sounds suddenly filled the dining room and ceased just as abruptly.

In the early part of this century, the vicar of the Abbey Church at Beaulieu, Revd Robert Powles, was to tell Lord Montagu's elder sister, Mrs Elizabeth Varley who grew up at Palace House, that he held a special midnight mass on Christmas Eve for the monks to attend, not so much for the repose of their souls it seems, but because he welcomed

them as members of his congregation. Mrs Varley said that she knew Mr Powles well. "He always appeared perfectly sane but he seemed to be on good terms with the ghosts whom he saw and spoke to regularly." The year 1940 saw the death of Revd Powles who had been the faithful incumbent of the Abbey Church at Beaulieu. Over the six decades that he held this post he came to accept the ghostly monks as part of his daily life and described them to many as going about their business with an air of friendliness. He treated them with reverence just as they did him and this he said with complete conviction.

The Cistercians grew vines at the Abbey and the present vineyard is the sight of another monastic haunting as visitors reported seeing a monk during the day towards the end of 1979

Among the many apparitions that have been recorded at Beaulieu is that of Isabella, Countess of Beaulieu, who died in 1786. She has been seen and heard many times walking to the private apartments and generally making a lot of noise.

A tenant in one of the houses near the Abbey was one night to experience unaccountable footsteps, loud bangs and crashes. That same night she had a dream in which a man came into her hall and confessed to killing another man in the wood. He had cut off his head and his hand and buried them outside the precinct wall, but now he wanted them buried inside the walls. He gave her directions to the place where she was to dig and as well as the remains, she would find two pebbles, one of which she should give to the Abbot and the other she was to keep. Unfortunately, it was not possible to dig in this place. The unexplained activity continued, so a seance was held by Sir Arthur Conan Doyle in which the ghost identified himself as 'De Ceignual'. Conan Doyle told him to depart in peace and the footsteps and the crashes ceased.

Bucklers Hard, a small village near Beaulieu, was to play its part in World War Two by hosting a small anti-aircraft detachment. One afternoon whilst off duty, two officers were driving past the Abbey when they encountered a small group of monks entering the grounds. It was two days before they could see the local vicar, who also acted as their service chaplain, and ask him to which order the monks belonged. Smiling, the vicar replied that the Beaulieu monks were Cistercians, but there had been none there since 1538. The somewhat bewildered officers found it hard to believe that they had been seeing apparitions of yesteryear, so the next day they returned to Beaulieu and ascertained beyond doubt that no mortal monks had visited on the day they saw them.

However, let us leave Beaulieu on a happier note with a story concerning the present Lord Montagu. His father was married towards the end of the 19th century and, in due course, five daughters were born to him. Naturally, he wished for a son to carry on the name and the traditions of the 5,000 acre estate. When at last he had a son he was overjoyed.

Not only was the proud father delighted, but at the moment of the boy's birth, all the swans on the lake and river rose into the air and flew in an excited flock round and round the house, as if to welcome the newcomer.

Dame Alicia Returns to Winchester

JAMES, Duke of Monmouth, the illegitimate son of Charles II and Lucy Walter, was born in Amsterdam in 1649. He became the idol of the populace thanks to his humanity towards the Scottish Covenantors until the Earl of Shaftesbury enmeshed him in the Rye House Plot in 1683 and he fled back to the Netherlands. On the death of Charles II in concert with a Scottish expedition by the 9th Duke of Argyle, together with 82 loyal followers, he landed at Lyme Regis, branded King James a 'popish usurper' and asserted his own legitimacy and right to the Crown. At Taunton, Somerset, his followers proclaimed him the rightful King James II and on 6 July 1685 they attempted, with 2,600 on foot and 600 on horses, to surprise James II encamped on Sedgemoor near Bridgewater. His men were mown down by the artillery and Monmouth fled, but was captured in a ditch near Ringwood, Hampshire. When he was brought before the king he wept, pleading for his life, and even offered to become a Catholic, but on 15 July 1685 after a trial and conviction, he was beheaded on Tower Hill, leaving his followers to be pursued and persecuted in the Bloody Assizes of Judge Jeffreys.

On the 4 September 1685, Dame Alicia Lisle was moved into a room overlooking a platform which had been erected in front of the Eclipse Inn. On this platform stood the block on which she would have to lay her head to await the the final retribution. Her crime? She had given refuge to two of Lord Monmouth's rebels.

Dame Alicia was the owner of the Elizabethan Moyles Court, one of Cromwell's staunchest supporters and an extremely forceful lady. She had married one of Cromwell's lords but later was to change her allegiance to the cause of the Royalists. When Monmouth's defeated rebel army fled, Dame Alicia took pity on two troopers and hid them at Moyles Court, one in the malthouse and the other in a priests' hole, but there was a traitor in her midst who betrayed her and Dame Alicia was arrested and tried for high treason.

She appeared before the notorious Judge Jeffreys at Winchester Castle where he cursed and raved at this frail old lady. Her sentence is regarded as being one of the most barbarous sentences ever to be passed on a lady of advanced years, for Jeffreys ordered that she should be placed on a hurdle and

The Eclipse Inn at Winchester.

dragged through the streets of Winchester to a place of execution, where she would then be burned alive, and he demanded the execution should take place that very day.

The horrified clergy of Winchester begged for a five-day postponement, placing the Judge under so much pressure that he relented and agreed.

During this time pleas were made to James II that the sentence should be reduced. The pleas stated that it was neither right or fitting that an old woman should be put to death in such a barbaric manner for what, after all was merely an act of mercy. The king agreed and reduced it to a sentence befitting a lady of her status – that of beheading. The scaffolding was erected against the timbered front of the old inn and it is said that Dame Alicia Lisle, this 71-year-old gentlewoman, spent her last night laying motionless on her bed, staring at the block. At the appointed hour the next morning, 5 September 1685, the axeman performed his duty and the sentence was duly carried out.

Ever since that day the Eclipse Inn has been haunted by a tall motionless figure in grey, seen by visitors in bedrooms, servants in hallways, and it is also

Doug and Sheila Cook, landlord and landlady of the Eclipse Inn.

reported that a servant was brushing carpets on one of the landings when she experienced a feeling that someone was watching her. Stopping work and glancing round she saw, standing in a dark corner of the landing a woman in a dark grey woollen dress. No features could be distinguished – it was just the figure of a woman. As the time was only 10am, the servant soldiered bravely on for the rest of her working day. However, some days later she was again to see the figure, in the same passageway and at the same hour, but this time it advanced and brushed against her, giving a gentle push. She called out, but nobody was there. She subsequently admitted that although the experience was extremely uncanny, she did not feel frightened.

Some American visitors to the inn told how they had seen a lady dressed in grey walking in the passageway and that same night were woken by the sound of rough voices and hammering outside, as if a structure were being hastily built.

Could this apparition be that of Dame Alicia Lisle, so brutally put to death for what was no more than an act of charity? Could the hammering sound have been attributed to the scaffold being built? We know that our American friends were in the same room in which Lady Lisle had spent her fateful last night on earth. As I sat drinking coffee in the bar of the Eclipse Inn, I asked Doug and Sheila Cook, present landlords, if they had witnessed the ghost or had experienced anything supernatural during their tenancy.

"Well, I haven't actually seen the ghost," replied Sheila, "However, when we first took over I was supervising the installation of a new cooker in the kitchen. For this purpose we had one of the interior walls pulled down. While this work was being carried out I walked from the kitchen into the bar. A few minutes later I was surprised to find that a water tap had been turned on in the kitchen. I know I was not responsible. It was certainly not running when I left to come into the bar and in order to turn it on whoever did so would have been forced to come behind the bar and push past me. I quickly went back, turned it off and once again returned to the bar. Later, when going back to the kitchen to get something from the freezer, the way had been blocked by a chair. The entrance is directly behind where I was standing in the bar but I neither saw or heard anything."

Both Doug and Sheila intimated that Dame Alicia may have been suspicious and worried as to their intentions for the Inn, but probably after ascertaining that no great alterations would be carried out she was satisfied and has not been seen or heard since.

Mentioning that the manager lived on the premises, Doug continued, "When we first came here we suggested that the top room, occupied by the unfortunate lady the night before her execution, together with the room next to it, could be turned into a self-contained flat for him. He was at first quite wary of living in these rooms, but eventually accepted. As far as I am aware he has never seen or experienced the ghost of Dame Alicia. At least if he has, he certainly hasn't said anything to us!"

It had never occurred to me that it was possible a spectre could haunt two different places, or in fact a series of places, but it is reported that Dame Alicia Lisle has been seen many times at Moyles Court, her old home on the outskirts of Ringwood, and in a driver-less coach in many places along the 15-mile route to the village of Dibden and the house of her son, where she had rested shortly before her arrest. Her apparition, minus head, is mostly seen in the coach which is being drawn by a large black horse. The horse is also minus its head.

During the investigation into her background it was interesting to find that the Lisles as a family originated from Wootton on the Isle of Wight. Dame Alicia's husband was Sir John Lisle, a strong adherent of Oliver Crom-

well who was assassinated at Lausanne many years before Alicia's execution. Here I would like to quote from a book by Ethel C. Hargrove first published in 1913.

'His wife, Alicia was long after beheaded, by order of the infamous Judge Jeffreys, for unwittingly sheltering two of Monmouth's soldiers, after the battle of Sedgemoor. Falsely accused of high treason, her great age was no protection against the terrible fate that befell her.

'Sir William Lisle, on the contrary, was a faithful Cavalier who followed Charles II into exile and is buried at Wootton. Wootton Lodge, formerly The Parsonage, is reputed to be haunted by the ghost of Dr Thomas Lisle, once Rector, who every night as the clock struck 12 ascended the stairs in his cassock and cap. It is strange that ghosts of the Lisle family should have been recorded through the annals of time to be haunting three or four different locations. Surely this must be a phenomenon in its own right.'

Winchester, the one time capital of England, is a city steeped in history, a place which saw the burial of St Swithin, whose skull, it is said was moved to Canterbury in the 11th century, one of his arms to Peterborough and the other to Stavaanger Cathedral in Norway.

With so much history, it is no wonder that a phantom monk has been seen so many times walking the aisles of the great Cathedral and mounting invisible

The grounds of Winchester Cathedral.

The west aisle of Winchester Cathedral.

steps. It is stated that photographs of spectres have been taken within the Cathedral confines. William the Conquerer owned a house in Winchester which was situated near the Cathedral. This house is still a place of mystery, a house where many inexplicable sounds are heard which seem to emanate from the very walls. A one-ime owner when questioned about the noises would look up and reply.: "Oh. That's only William again"

But for the owner's little pomeranian dog it would have been a different story, for she would lay, trembling with fear, as if seeing an unseen visitor. One night,

however, a guest was woken suddenly. Her bedchamber was an old panelled room and the sound which caused her to wake was akin to someone stumbling into the panelling and the cupboards and knocking into the skirting boards. Transfixed with fear she lay there until morning.

At first light she bade a hasty farewell to her host and vowed never to return to the house again.

When thinking of hauntings our thoughts always seem to turn to times gone by, but there is a recorded story of the haunting of a Winchester council house. Mrs Joyce Bowles was to find herself in the ghostly presence of an elderly man, a lady in white and a nun. This occurred on numerous occasions. At one time she was talking to her next-door neighbour who suddenly found that she could not move her feet. In fact she was rooted to the spot, but Joyce could see a man in black standing behind her

The old arch in the grounds of Winchester Cathedral, thought to mark the site of the burial place of St Swithin.

friend, a long black cloak across his shoulders fastened at the neck by a chain and two brass buttons. When the ghost moved on, the neighbour's legs regained their normal usage. Other friends have witnessed the movement of furniture in the bedrooms of this haunted house at 45 Quarry Road. Mattresses have moved, apparently by themselves. It fell to the Revd Ramsdale Whalley, the official exorcist to the Diocese of Winchester, to seek out the poltergeist and hold a service of exorcism but without success. It is reported that Mrs Ann Strickland, Renee and Tom Platt and a Mrs Shears saw many objects, from candlesticks to books, moving as if propelled by unseen hands.

The Bowles family, with their four sons, having never taken any interest in ghosts, were only too pleased when in 1968 they were offered a chance to move into a three-bedroomed semi-detatched house.

They had not been there long before a poltergeist was heard roaming the house calling the name 'Joyce'. Mrs Bowles went from room to room in an attempt to find out whence the voice came but finally went to bed alone, as her husband was on night shift at Winchester station. Slowly she drifted into a well-deserved slumber, only to be disturbed by the sound of heavy footsteps walking around her bed. She felt a great pressure on her chest and was struggling to get her breath, at the same time having the impression that she was being lifted several inches above the bed. As she struggled, she was conscious of the church clock striking midnight. The street lighting was extinguished, leaving the room in total darkness, and at the same time the pressure was released and she seemed to float back to her bed.

She lay there unable to pluck up courage to venture downstairs until the first rays of dawn.

On another occasion Joyce was to see a figure of a nun complete with white head dress and a young pleasant face.

These hauntings were to continue for many years and by the autumn of 1973 Joyce Bowles was beginning to imagine herself mentally ill, but was assured by doctors and other people who had witnessed strange things that there was nothing wrong with her mental state. It was her milkman who finally convinced her of this when he recalled the morning when he was enjoying a cup of coffee and had seen one of the armchairs lift itself from the floor and slide across the room.

Radio and TV reporters interviewing Joyce for a local programme found that their equipment was mysteriously affected and one one of the crew slumped into a trance like state. When he regained consciousness he reported seeing a vision of robed people singing. Needless to say, he did not remain for long.

It seems strange, to say the least, that most apparitions seem to haunt properties, whereas the poltergeist would prefer to attach itself to a person. But whatever the ghostly apparition may be, whether poltergeist or friendly spirit, certainly the city of Winchester seems to have its fair share. On the outskirts of the city is Golden Common and the manor house at Marwell, the grounds of which are now a zoo.

There have been suggestions that the marriage of King Henry VIII to Jane Seymour took place in secret at Marwell Hall prior to the execution of Anne Boleyn, and that the apparition which walks the rooms and corridors at Marwell is that of Jane.

Marwell has had a chequered history. The house originally belonged to the church, its administration being under the auspices of the Bishops of Winchester until it was given to Sir Henry Seymour by a grateful monarch.

In the early part of the 16th century, the house was owned by Sir Thomas Seymour who was a violent man with great ambition and thought little of turning against his brother, Edward, in an attempt to gain further popularity with Henry VIII. On the death of the

Marwell Manor, Golden Common, near Winchester.

king he sought the position of guardian of the young King Edward VI, but without success. He then aspired to the hand of Princess Elizabeth, the king's sister, later to become Queen Elizabeth I. Again frustrated, he was to settle on secretly marrying Catherine Parr, the late king's widow, and on her death once more turned his attentions to the young Princess Elizabeth, thus incurring the extreme displeasure of both her and the Court. He was executed on 20 March 1549.

It is these events and many more like them that have given Marwell Hall the reputation of being pervaded with a constant aura of sadness over the centuries. When it was rebuilt in the mid-19th century it was said that it was spoilt in many ways, but having no plans or drawings of the old house there is nothing with which to compare it. There still remains the enormous carved Seymour fireplace, and the ancient Royal Arms, once affixed over the imposing front entrance are now to be seen in the hall. There have been seen many unidentified ancestral ghosts over the years, not only in the form of apparitions, but heavy footsteps have been heard in the many corridors and on the stairways, and secret hideaways have been discovered, reported to have been used by long since departed smugglers. There also exists a story that when Henry VIII gave the property to Sir Henry Seymour, the local priest considered it to be an act of theft from the church and cursed the entire Seymour family and their descendants with bell, book and candle, using all the power at his command. His curse was that they would lose the house and estates and even the very line of Seymour. On hearing this, the king had the priest dragged from the church where he was saying Mass at the altar and put to death immediately without trial. Henry's own three grandsons were the last of the line to bear the name Seymour – so, did the curse come true?

One of the places in which apparitions are reported mostly to appear is the Yew Tree Walk, an extremely pretty avenue of well established yew trees situated to the north-west of the hall. There, the ghostly apparition of a lady dressed in white was often to be seen, and many say that this is the ghost of Anne Boleyn seeking revenge on Henry's lover, Jane Seymour.

There is a legend concerning the Yew Tree Walk. It led to a green door which opened on to the Owslebury Road and it is said that, should the door ever be blocked, the surrounding brickwork would fall. If one looks today, this is just what has happened, for now, reliable accounts of the sightings are few. Is there, maybe, some connection?

Sweet Fanny Adams of Alton

OVER a pair of cottages in Amery Street is a plaque which states that Edmund Spenser lived there in 1590 before he was married.

Spenser, 'Prince of Poets' and friend of Sir Walter Raleigh was to write the immortal *Faerie Queene* which he dedicated to Queen Elizabeth I. It was Sir Walter who first presented Spenser to Court. He was to change the standard sonnet so beloved of all the poets of that era to the stanza of nine lines, consisting of eight ten-syllable lines and a final Alexandrine which is a line consisting of six iambics with a caesura after the third. This style was first used in a poem to Alexander the Great in the year 323BC, and this was to cause him to became known as the Poets' Poet and a favourite of all. Spenser and Raleigh it is said, often compared their writings, for Raleigh was to write accounts of his explorations of

The grave of Fanny Adams in Alton Cemetery.

the eastern seaboard of America and considered himself to be a fair poet.

It has often been said that in some ways, the sudden death of Edmund Spenser in 1599 was a blessing in disguise for him, as in all probability he could have been pulled into the misfortunes which beset Raleigh when he was convicted of conspiracy against James I in 1603, only to be reprieved but eventually executed by James in 1618.

The two cottages were once a single house and in the vicinity there are often sightings of Edmund, dressed in Elizabethan garb and absorbed in his Spenserian stanza. John Aubrey, antiquarian writer of the 17th century, was to put pen to paper and write of this apparition: 'Enjoyed his muse, in this delicate sweet air, and writ a good part of his verse.'

Even to this day there are many sightings of this Elizabethan gentleman.

Let us now move on to

St Lawrence Church, Alton.

1858, in which year Alton saw the birth of Fanny Adams, who was so savagely murdered in the ninth year of her life. A local solicitor's clerk, Frederick Baker, was accused of her brutal murder. After his arrest a subsequent search of his house brought to light his diary, the entry for that fatal day, Saturday, 24 August 1867 read: 'Killed a young girl. It was fine and hot.'

He was brought before Mr Justice Mellor at Winchester Assizes, held at Winchester Castle and tried for the wilful murder of the girl. The prosecution proved beyond all reasonable doubt that he had callously killed Fanny Adams and dismembered her young pathetic body in a field near her home. The subsequent execution of Frederick Baker was proclaimed with the following announcement:

'At the appointed time he was conducted to the scaffold and after a few minutes spent in prayer he was launched into eternity.'

Over the years there have been many sightings of poor, unfortunate Fanny. The spectre of this sweet little girl is often seen playing in and around the fields where she was so brutally murdered. There are times when people have been able to sit watching her making daisy chains, and other times when she is seen just skipping through the long grass. Many people have tried to make contact with Fanny, but on their approach the apparition simply fades into thin air.

To this day this small girl's name has been immortalised and is in daily use, for at the time of her murder the Royal Navy was in the throes of changing the shipboard staple diet from hard biscuit to tinned meat. Macabre as it may be, the sailors were to liken the contents of the tins to the remains of the unfortunate Fanny Adams and so, into our modern language came the saying 'Sweet Fanny Adams' to mean 'There is

The fireplace at the Crown Inn, Alton, now the Crown Hotel.

nothing in it'. Another haunting to beset Alton was at the Crown Inn in the centre of town. It is the sound of a dog barking, scratching and whining, though no dog ever materialised.

Superstition has it that a cruel owner, displeased with his dog, was to smash its head against a brick fireplace in the dining room and throw the body into the fire. Shortly after the incident the fireplace was bricked up.

In 1967, the then owners decided to instigate alterations which necessitated the removal of the false wall covering the original dining room hearth. There was discovered the skeleton of a dog. After a decent interment for these grisly remains, the ghostly barking was to cease. The dog was not the only ghost that was to haunt the inn, for there have been many sightings of an apparition of a female wearing the garb of a maidservant of years gone by, but no light can be shed as to who she was or even as to the reason why she can find no rest but haunts the inn during autumn.

The church of St Lawrence is known

St Lawrence Church, showing damage caused during the English Civil War.

Close-up of bullet holes in the door of St Lawrence Church.

Oliver Cromwell's house at Alton.

as a local landmark with its many carvings of such diverse animals from dragons to doves and asses to hyenas. There have been many reported noisy ghosts in the church itself as if the battles that took place there during the civil war were still being fought.

It is known that the Royalist Colonel Boles made a stand there against the powerful Cromwellian troopers under the leadership of Sir William Whaller and many bullet marks are still to be seen on the pillars and door of the church.

Visitors have at various times stated that they became so immersed in the atmosphere that they actually felt the struggling and fighting men and heard the sounds of the battle that took place some 300 years ago.

Could it be that those unfortunate wretches who inflicted death upon another on consecrated ground can find no rest?

Love-sick Nurses of Netley Hospital

DURING the 111 years of its existence, the Royal Victoria Military Hospital, Netley, was regarded by those in authority as a 'ghastly construction' and described by many as a most unsuitable building for the purpose. Due to much public and even official criticism, Netley Hospital became the subject of an official enquiry which resulted in the Ministry of Defence referring to it as 'a scandal'.

Her Majesty, Queen Victoria, laid the foundation stone at the inauguration of the hospital in 1856. At the opening ceremony the queen, who was staying at her Isle of Wight home, Osborne House, was reported as saying that she thought often of her poor brave soldiers and those who returned injured, who would be able to receive every comfort during the time of their hospitalisation at Netley.

To a certain extent this was true, as the establishment successfully treated up to 800 military personnel at any one time, and during World War Two this figure was to be exceeded many times over. Netley Hospital would often be regarded by patients and staff alike as a cheerless and unhappy building, Florence Nightingale once describing it as 'a hateful place with no atmosphere'.

From the days of that esteemed lady and her heroic exploits in the Crimean War to its demolition in 1967, Netley Hospital was haunted by an apparition which always manifested itself in the same part of the building. It is reported that the ghost was that of a nurse of the time, dressed in a uniform of the period, a combination of grey and blue with a white cap. The apparition seemed not to notice those who were near but would silently and slowly glide along in the direction of the hospital chapel where it would vanish into thin air. Its appearance always seemed to be a warning that a death was imminent and, according to reports, the apparition was never wrong.

More recently, a night duty telephone switchboard operator who had been working at Netley for nearly 30 years said, "I once saw the ghost and smelt a strong perfume. At the same time, a night nurse saw the same spectre pass along a corridor next to the telephone room in which I was on duty. True to form, one of her patients died the next morning."

Over the years many theories as to the origin of the ghost have been put forward. One of the most popular suggestions

The Royal Victoria Hospital at Netley.

seems to be that the apparition is of a nurse during the Crimean War who accidentally gave a patient an incorrect dose of strong drugs which caused his death. Soon afterwards, being unable to live with her conscience, the young nurse committed suicide by jumping out of a top floor window. This incident is well documented in hospital records.

Another theory is that during the Crimean War a nurse fell in love with a patient. The rule strongly discouraging emotional involvement between staff and patients was apparently the same then as it is now. However, it is reported that the patient did not reciprocate her feelings. To make matters worse for the lovesick nurse, she learned that the young soldier was rather keen on a colleague. She poisoned him and then swallowed a fatal dose of drugs. This theory is hypothetical in that no evidence or reports are available in what can only be described as an excellently kept set of records.

The third theory, maybe even more unbelievable is that the spectre was Florence Nightingale herself. It was seen rather more frequently during the 1960s when plans were afoot to demolish the

Nursing staff at Netley in 1897, with their superintendent, Miss Norman.

place. Although our great heroine was never fond of Netley, her expertise and advice was taken when the building was originally designed.

Was this dedicated lady sad at the thought of it being demolished?

Be this, or any other of the suggestions, as it may, the Royal Victoria Military Hospital was demolished in 1967 and the ghost has never been seen since. Hopefully she may have now found eternal peace.

Southampton's Stones of Terror

AS I commence this chapter about Southampton and probably the most complicated and horrific herein, I must confess experiencing some difficulty when trying to compare an evil manifestation from the Northumberland town of Hexham in parallel with the peaceful campus of Southampton University. The only possible way to answer such a problem is to return to the very beginning of these bizarre happenings and report them as they were related to me.

It started in the garden of a council house in Hexham and the events occurred comparatively recently in the annals of ghostly happenings, in fact just 23 years ago.

A gardener, digging an overgrown patch of waste ground at the end of the garden, unearthed two stone heads. They were grossly ugly, worn in places with thick necks and evil looking features, not the sort of pieces with which most people would grace their mantleshelf or cabinet. But the gardener, thinking they may be of some value, took them into the house and suggested that the tenant, a lady with two small children, had them valued.

Neighbours living in adjoining council houses became worried and somewhat suspicious when they failed to see the good lady or her children. They noted that milk was still on the doorstep, although the front door was open. Deciding to check that all was well with the family, one of them entered the house.

The tenant was in a complete state of agitation, her speech incoherent and babbling that she had 'seen the devil'. The neighbours soon took the lady and the two young children and settled them in an adjoining property while they searched the house, but all seemed normal. As far as could be ascertained. nothing was amiss.

On completion of the search, they found that the good lady had recovered sufficiently and was able to relate what she had seen. She said.

"It began with a very strange noise. Then the wind seemed to blow and a terrifying shape appeared. It wasn't animal or human. Wherever I went in the house it seemed to follow me."

At this point no one had equated the two heads resting on the kitchen window sill with the evil apparition.

So traumatic was her experience that on the recommendation of her medical practitioner, the local council rehoused the family. During the move, when asked what she wanted done with the two heads, she suggested that they be sent to the local museum. This stage in the narrative fetches us back to Hampshire and the campus of Southampton University. The Hexham museum, being unable to date or locate the origin of the two heads decided to send them for analysis to the archæological and pagan studies department of a university.

The university chosen was Southampton. I was able to speak to the archæologist at a later date and due to the bizarre happenings associated with these heads, she has asked me not to reveal her name. For the purposes of this report therefore, I will use the pseudonym 'Dr June'.

It is reported that Dr June took an instant dislike to the heads, although at the time having no idea what they were. She experienced a cold atmosphere and an uncanny feeling of terror.

At the time she was extremely busy, so decided to take the heads home. On arrival she placed them in a cupboard with some other items which she was in the process of examining. In the middle of the night she found herself suddenly awake and bathed in perspiration, accompanied by a feeling of terror. She was cold, although it was a balmy summer night. Getting out of bed and turning towards the door she saw standing there, a giant shape, half animal, half human. She reported that it was bent over, had the head of a dog and was covered with fur.

She stood up, the terror rising within her when the apparition left the bedroom and moved towards the stairs. As if mes-

merised, the archaeologist was compelled to follow. As the creature reached the halfway point it leapt over the bannister and rushed through the kitchen towards the back door where it inexplicably vanished.

As the feeling of terror subsided and the atmosphere returned to normal, the doctor rushed to check that all the doors were still safely locked, then quickly returning to the bedroom, woke her husband. Reluctantly, as one just roused from sleep, he listened to the story and went to inspect the kitchen. Erring on the side of safety he also checked the other parts of the house but could see no sign of any such creature having entered the premises. They both agreed that they would not discuss it further as their children, a teenage girl and an infant boy, had appeared to sleep through it all. Because of her extreme dislike of her latest acquisitions, Dr June decided to deal with them first which would mean their remaining in the house for only about another week. But during this time several other inexplicable terrors were manifest.

The day after she had seen the figure at the door of her bedroom, she was working when suddenly a strong gust of wind rushed along the hallway and burst through into the study, forcing open the door. She saw nothing, but the cat, up to now asleep on the rug, suddenly awoke and fur bristling, the animal slowly backed through the door, tail bushed. Going to comfort her, Dr June found that she was trembling from head to toe. It was many days before she ventured back into the study, which hitherto had been her favourite room.

A few days later, Dr June and her husband were called away for the day on business, telling the children that they would be home early that evening. On arrival they found their daughter looking pale and distraught. When questioned she said that she had been feeling unwell all day and would soon go to bed. Whilst her mother went to prepare a meal in the kitchen, the daughter, not wishing to cause alarm told her father what was wrong.

She said that, on arriving from school she opened the front door and came face to face with what she could only describe as a 'wolf like creature', which had bounded halfway up the stairs, jumped over the bannister and rushed towards the rear of the house. She could not explain her feelings, but although panic stricken knew the urgent need to follow. It vanished when reaching the kitchen. Knowing that her mother was pregnant she begged her father not to say anything which may cause any alarm.

Some days later, having completed her examination of the heads, the doctor was able to report her findings.

Recently she told me: "As you know, these heads came from the border town of Hexham, a town renowned for artifacts from a pagan past. We know that in the seventh century there was an Anglo Saxon church which housed a Roman tombstone and the 'Frith Stool', once the throne of Saxon bishops. Later, on the

same site was built an Augustinian Priory Church. That was in about the 12th or 13th centuries, and, of course, nearby on Hadrian's Wall we have Housesteads Roman Fort where many of these artifacts have been found and have since been housed in the museum there. So it came as no surprise to me when I learned that the two heads had been unearthed in a Hexham garden."

She said that she had no knowledge that the apparitions had appeared to the council house tenant in Hexham, the previous holder of these heads. Indeed, she would have been reluctant to introduce them into her household had this been so. Subsequently, however, she discovered that, after the gardener placed the heads on a window sill in the kitchen of the council house, that same evening, when the lady was saying goodnight to her baby, the front door burst open to reveal a creature, half man half beast which, jumping at her, knocked her out of its way. In doing so it collided with the baby's cot, knocking it across the room. In the kitchen, it vanished. For the next few days the tenant was in a bad state and subsequently suffered a mild nervous breakdown. The doctor had also been told by the Hexham authorities that the council had rehoused the family and that the heads were taken to the local museum.

Dr June continued: "As I have always been a believer in the paranormal and supernatural, when the Hexham museum sent the heads to me for analysis, I had an immediate feeling that they radiated evil.

I cannot describe this feeling, but assure you it is one of the most ghastly that any human can ever experience. At least, it seemed so to me. However, I am fortunate in that I have a firm religious faith which helped me overcome the dreadful manifestations I witnessed."

Leaving her report she went on to tell me about other work she had on the shelf where she had placed the two heads. One of these pieces was also a stone bust of a devil.

"It was a horrible little thing which in itself represented evil. It may seem silly but its eyes seemed to change in size. Sometimes the right eye would be twice the size of the left, then the next night it would be the other way round." I think we must take into account the fact that we are not quoting an irrational person, but a trained professional archaeologist, one who has made a career in the study of artifacts from around the world and civilisations spanning many centuries.

After experiencing the apparitions and now in possession of the details of those experienced by the tenant of the council house, they decided that a local priest who was also a mutual friend, would ask a Catholic priest who was an trained exorcist to attend a meeting. At this meeting he was introduced to the bust of the 'little devil'. Placing his hand on the bust he immediately reeled back saying that it was an evil thing which had been used in sacrifices and should be removed from the house as soon as possible, for not only did it exude evil, but also was capable of absorbing it.

The next day being Sunday, no one was in a hurry to rouse from their slumbers. However, the doctor's five-year-old son somewhat tearfully went to wake his mother. And here I quote: "We had told him nothing of the apparitions which both my daughter and I had witnessed. After climbing on to my bed he said, 'I just went downstairs to get a glass of juice and as I came out of the playroom a funny black thing was there and it was like half a wolf and half a man. It jumped upstairs ahead of me and went in to the spare bedroom. I didn't want to, but I had to follow it.' I tried to comfort him by suggesting that perhaps it was just a shadow or something like that but he was so sure of what he had seen and I found it no mean thing to try to explain, for his only answer was 'Oh no, it wasn't a shadow. There was something funny about it'."

Later that day her next door neighbour stated that she was a psychic person and said, "You have evil in your house and you must get rid of it at once – and by that I mean today, not tomorrow for that will be too late."

That night Dr June was to experience a severe miscarriage which nearly proved fatal and her recovery took many weeks. Her husband immediately returned the two stone heads to the museum at Hexham and everybody felt that a great cloud had been lifted from their lives.

On her return to work there was much correspondence regarding the incidents of paranormality which they had all experienced. One letter was from a professional man living in Hexham, who told her that he had been speaking to one of his lorry drivers earlier that morning. This driver had heard about the heads and admitted that they were made by him some years ago, essentially to amuse his young daughter. Others detailed the passage of the heads since leaving her house and being returned to Hexham.

At first the museum did not want them and suggested they be returned, but her husband categorically refused to have them back in the house. It was then suggested that they be re-interred in the garden whence they originally came and the new tenant of the council house readily agreed. This was duly done, but that night the tenant experienced the same spectre – a half human and half beast creature. In the morning she was still hysterical and pleaded with her husband to dig them up again and throw them away.

Her sister-in-law, dismissing the idea as a lot of 'fairy stories' and 'complete nonsense', asked if she could have them to take home as ornaments for her mantleshelf. That night the same fate befell her.

At about this time, Dr June had embarked on a series of lectures and by sheer coincidence met the lorry driver who had claimed the making of the heads. A little sceptical, she asked him if he would make her a duplicate for her records and send it to her in order that she would be able to compare. He agreed and they parted company. A few weeks later

the head duly arrived and she said. "The head which he had made was nothing like the original. In fact, a child could possibly have done better."

I asked her from where in her opinion the heads originated, she stated.

"I'm not exactly sure. They are certainly much too old to have been made by the lorry driver, for they are pagan in origin. I would give a considered opinion that they were a symbol used for ancient pagan worship, at somewhere like the old Abbey Church, or at Housesteads. There was an altar there you know."

I asked her where the heads were now and she replied: "As far as I know, they are with an eminent psychic scientist in London who is researching into their origins. His theory is that they have been the subject of emotional Satanic worship which re-manifests itself. As far as I can ascertain they are still somewhere in London to this day. The one thing I do know is that I will never allow them again to come into my house or into contact with my family."

During my drive home from my interview I contemplated what had been said to me and what I knew already.

Because of this apparition, one family had moved house. An eminent doctor of archaeology left her post and moved to another part of the country. What I failed to understand was, why a lorry driver should claim to have made two such evil effigies. Maybe he wanted self glory such as one who confessed to a murder knowing full well they had not committed it.

Of Phantom Ships and Sailors

THE old adage 'ships that pass in the night' applies to the waters of the Solent more than most. Here we may be forgiven for changing this to 'the ghost ships that pass in the day or night'.

With the amount of shipping using the narrow but treacherous waters from Spithead to Hurst Point and the dangerous rocky shores of the Southern Wight, there have been many wrecks and tragedies over the centuries.

One story which cannot be omitted in any book dealing with apparitions at sea is the tragedy of HMS *Eurydice*, a naval training ship wrecked in the year 1878 off Dunnose Point, Isle of Wight. Since then she has been the subject of numerous sightings and is still seen to this day.

Built in the early 1840s, this two-decked fully-rigged sailing frigate with excellent sea-going qualities not to be found in many other ships of the day, was a favourite with all who sailed in her. *Eurydice* was converted into a training ship in 1877, being stripped of her guns and fitted with extra cabin and store space. Her newly-appointed commander, The Hon Marcus Hare, was an experienced captain, having served in other training ships, and prior to this

had commanded many other RN ships. A popular officer, he gained much respect from his fellow officers and crew.

After the refit was completed in Portsmouth, *Eurydice* left on her first (and as it turned out, only) training cruise to the West Indies. On board were many new recruits and the usual complement of experienced crew.

After spending the next few months in the Caribbean working in conjunction with two other training ships, the *Martin* and the *Liberty*, Capt Hare received instructions to take *Eurydice* to Bermuda to embark 60 passengers, mainly army officers returning to Britain. On 6 March *Eurydice* finally left for home, entering the English Channel on 14 March.

Capt Hare chose to round the Isle of Wight along the south side before entering Portsmouth Harbour. A report from the coastguard stated that she was approaching Dunnose Point at 15.30 under full sail and he wrote the following in his log: 'It was obvious that Capt Hare intended to dock at Portsmouth before nightfall.'

It was Sunday and as was the custom in the Royal Navy, most of the crew were relaxing. Some were asleep down below and others reading, writing letters or even catching up on minor sewing or darning jobs. With the passengers the ship was rather crowded and in order to ventilate her, two of the gun ports were opened. Even those on watch were not busy, some were just looking at the Island and distant shores of Portsmouth, glad, no doubt to be home.

On shore, old sailors, remembering their days under sail, and parties of walkers hurrying to keep warm in the low temperature and steadily rising wind, looked at the full-sailed *Eurydice* in awe. However, it has since transpired from the records that even the hikers, most of whom were not old salts, remarked that, for the strength of the wind at the time, she was carrying too much sail. In fact, one of them wrote a letter to *The Times* casting doubt upon Capt Hare's seamanship; but those on board *Eurydice* were sheltered by the cliffs and temporarily enjoying calm waters, therefore they would have been ignorant of the rising wind and the dark clouds approaching from the north-west.

I will now crave your indulgence whilst I deviate slightly from the events which led to the next few minutes in the life and death of this fine ship.

I would like to quote from *Wanderings in the Isle of Wight,* written in 1913 by Ethel C.Hargrove, who witnessed the sinking of the *Eurydice* whilst playing with other children on the beach at Sandown at a spot then named Fisherman's Village.

In one chapter of her book in which she describes the building of the pier and the many changes taking place at the time she writes: 'I think all these changes were taking place about the time when the ill-fated *Eurydice* went down in sight of shore. I remember that Sunday afternoon with a shudder now; the sudden gust, a blinding blizzard, then silence, an empty space on the horizon where half an hour previously a ship in full sail, graceful as some white swan, was silhouetted against the grey sky. Later on, one could discern three masts, and finally her hulk was tugged under the lee of the Culvers. For years after the wreck was mentioned with bated breath, and it almost seemed to us children as though our playmate the sea had committed as unspeakable cruelty and when I beheld Lord Leighton's *The Sea Gave up her Dead* I thought of the *Eurydice.*"

During the whole of this book I have endeavoured to steer away from 'premonitions' which happen to many people as a general course of their day to day lives and can never really be explained. However, I feel that I must create a precedent in this case.'

Sitting in his comfortable house at Windsor, nearly 70 miles away, was retired government official Sir John MacNiell. He was, therefore, nowhere near Dunnose Point or the Isle of Wight, but was having tea with the Bishop of Ripon, Sir John Colwell, who reported that suddenly MacNiell rose from his chair, looked out of his window and said: "Good Heavens! Why don't they close the portholes and reef the topsails!" Until his dying day Colwell was bewildered and MacNiell was never able to explain what caused this momentary action and remark. All he was able to say was that in his minds eye he had a vision of a ship in the channel under full sail with her portholes open. Above was thick black cloud although at the time in Windsor it was brilliant sunshine. "I just had this feeling that the vessel was doomed." he said

Back at Dunnose Point *Eurydice* was beginning to sail out of the lee of the cliffs and the barometer began to fall alarmingly. Still no one was unduly perturbed as the slight breeze became merely moderate. It was not until she sailed away from the shelter of the cliffs, however, that her sails began to react to a sudden increase in wind.

Immediately Capt Hare appeared on deck and ordered his crew to reef, becoming concerned at the sudden rise in wind and the black cloud which by now had become a thick curtain of snow obliterating most of the shore line.

It was now clear that *Eurydice* was experiencing problems. The lighter sails would have to be furled. As this instruction was being carried out, the snow storm hit the ship and within minutes the amount of snow on the deck made crew movement difficult.

By now the ship was heeling dangerously to starboard and the helmsman reacted quickly to Capt Hare's orders to bring her closer to wind. This only had the effect of driving her deeper into the swell and more water began to come in through the open ports.

The crew were now beginning to panic and some tried to reach the companionway, only a few making it. *Eurydice* was now over at such an angle that high freezing waves broke over her, ripping out ladders, fixtures, fittings and trapping the starboard watch.

Knowing that *Eurydice* could not now be saved, Capt Hare gave orders to abandon ship with every man for himself, but it was too late. This fine ship had given up and was capsizing rapidly.

Some of the crew and passengers managed to throw themselves overboard but the freezing water would soon have taken its toll of those trying to make it to shore. Rescue ships were on the scene within half an hour, but most of the unfortunate victims had perished. In this short time over 300 men were drowned.

Research shows that there were only two survivors, Ordinary Seaman Fletcher and Able Seaman Cuddiford. They were both picked up by the schooner *Emma*, as by this time the snow had cleared and lookouts on board the *Emma* saw wreckage floating and heard the men's shouts. Relatives and friends, knowing that *Eurydice* was to arrive at Portsmouth during that Sunday, were gathering at the dockside eager to greet their sons and lovers who had been at sea for at least four months.

At a house in Gosport, Eleanor Lake, sister of a young midshipman David Bennett, together with her husband was preparing to welcome her brother home. David would always stay with them when in Portsmouth, bringing his sister and brother-in-law a present from afar.

After four months at sea there would be much news to catch up on. It was about 3.30pm that Eleanor began to feel an inexplicable anxiety. She was unable to describe the feeling which she experienced, but somehow she realised that something awful had happened. This she later confided to her husband and her family.

Suddenly she heard David's footsteps on the gravel path and, relieved that he was home at last, she began to dismiss her feeling of a few moments earlier. She opened the door to welcome him but no one was there.

She called and searched, looking along the street both ways, and it was then that the feeling of dread began to reoccur. At that moment she became certain that something had happened to her brother. Somehow she knew in her mind that he was dead. The following morning she had her worst fears confirmed when she and many others learned of the tragedy which had befallen *Eurydice.*

Although I have not been able to ascertain for certain, rumours over the 117 years have persisted that others also returned to their loved ones at their dying hour.

It was five months before the *Eurydice* was salvaged and by that time none of the bodies which went down with her were recognisable. Maybe they were granted that respite in order to warn their families that they were no longer

alive, hoping at least to ease some of the anguish which would have been felt had they been present at the salvaging.

But what of the ghost of *Eurydice* herself? Broken and smashed she may have been, but still she appears in all her full-sailed glory to haunt the waters around Dunnose Point. Local fisherman have often reported seeing a full-sailed ship bearing down on them at considerable speed, but as they took avoiding action, she just disappeared into thin air. People walking on the cliffs have stated categorically that they have seen her. A trick of light maybe, or some weird relection?

Most of the fishermen to this day swear that the apparition is the ghost of *Eurydice* – and fishermen in these parts are a hardy and stolid breed, far from being impractical and even less prone to exaggeration or flights of fancy.

One of the most reliable reports comes from a naval officer, Commander Frederick Lipscombe. He was the commander of a submarine which in the 1930s nearly collided with a man o' war at Dunnose Point. This is recorded in his ship's log.

He later decided to find out a little more and asked a number of Island residents. Their only explanation – and one which he accepted – was that this was the ghost of the *Eurydice.*

Of all professions, that of a seaman seems to carry with it the reputation of extreme superstition. I have known ships' captains who would spend another whole day waiting for tides,

rather than sail on the 13th. *Eurydice* left Bermuda for England on such a day. In fact, Friday 13th.

Was there any connection? I personally cannot see that a date makes any difference, but then, who am I to try to disprove the wisdom of our ancestors over generations? Maybe one day we will be given the answer.

Yarmouth

For another report of an apparition at sea we will travel to Yarmouth on the Isle of

The wreck of HMS *Gladiator.*

Wight. It was here that I spoke to Peter, a man in his late 50s who has lived for most of his life in Yarmouth. Peter's position in the community makes it important that I withhold his full name and therefore I am respecting his wishes.

Early one morning in the spring of 1958, Peter was on his way from Yarmouth to Freshwater with an interim call at Colwell Chine. He slowed the car as he approached the chine as the weather was extremely misty, the visibility down to about about 20 yards. As he glanced seaward out of the car window, he was surprised to see a large warship dating back to at least World War One. Being reared in this area Peter prides himself on his knowledge of things maritime and especially of the movements of shipping in this area of the Solent. Seeing a ship of that age his curiosity got the better of him and he stopped the car at the sea front in order to take a closer look.

"The ship was so near to the shore, I must admit that I had visions of her running aground in the mist. The channel between Hurst Point and Colwell is extremely narrow and I feared the worst," he said. As he approached the beach he was overcome by a terrible and inexplicable dread. He knew that he should go on, but at the same time had this feeling that he should not be there.

I asked him if he could describe what he saw in detail and he replied: "I vividly remember seeing figures on the foredeck apparently trying to throw something overboard. I got out of the car and walked as near as I could to the beach but as I approached – suddenly everything disappeared. It just vanished, melted away in the mist."

Knowing his reputation as a professional man I would not think of him as being easily scared, but Peter admitted: "I am generally of an extremely logical turn of mind and was, even at a tender age, but I must admit that I have never been so scared in the whole of my life, before or since, and yet, I really could not tell what I was so scared of.

"I just knew that I had to leave the scene. As far as I can recall, I just ran back to the car and was still shaking when I reached Freshwater."

I asked Peter if he had bothered to try to find an explanation for what he had seen and he continued: "Yes indeed. I certainly was not prepared to let the matter rest there. After some time and research I managed to find out that HMS *Gladiator*, a Royal Navy cruiser second class, was returning from Portland to her home base in Portsmouth when she was in collision with the steam ship *St Paul*, a massive liner, once the pride of America Lines. On 25 April 1908, the *St Paul* left Southampton Water and entered The Solent on a course which would take her along the north coast of the Isle of Wight and out through The Needles," he related.

Apparently it is reported that due to the mist the pilot, Capt George Bowyer ordered very much reduced speed through Hurst Point when suddenly another ship came into view. She was the *Gladiator*. Bowyer, knowing that for a ship the size of *St Paul*, stopping the engines would have little or no effect, signalled to *Gladiator* his intention of immediately putting the engines full astern.

On board *Gladiator*, Capt Lumsden RN suddenly became aware of the *St Paul* appearing to be advancing bow on. Uncertain what was going on, he ordered his engines stopped and steered '30 degrees starboard' which would have the effect of veering the *Gladiator* round to port. Although the rules of the sea when two vessels are heading for collision are to pass each other portside, there was just no room at this point for any such manoeuvre. The *St Paul* hit the *Gladiator*, her bow driving into the starboard side of the RN ship.

Capt Lumsden somehow steered the *Gladiator* towards the shore and beached her, and although she suffered badly, turning over on her side, miraculously, only 27 lives were lost. She was eventually salvaged and sold for scrap.

As for the *St Paul*, with the help of lifeboats and tugs she managed to make her way back to Southampton and dry dock where she was repaired and was in service before being scrapped 15 years later.

I asked Peter if he could reconcile this story with the mysterious happenings he saw on Colwell beach.

"It was many years before I was sure," he said. "I was in no way certain that I saw the *Gladiator* until I was reading a book entitled *Phantoms of the High Seas* by Phillip MacDougall. There he tells the story of these two ships in vivid detail with a photograph of the *Gladiator* when she was in dry dock after the accident.

"There is no doubt whatever in my mind that the ship I saw that day in April was the *Gladiator*. Since then I have knowledge of many reports of her being seen, and disappearing, just as she did that misty day. It seems to happen every ten years.

"I have never seen her before or since. In fact I am one of the least 'psychic' people you have probably interviewed, but I did not dream this experience. I often wonder why, 50 years later to the time and day, I should have been chosen to witness the supernatural. Would there be something in the fact that 25 April is my birthday?"

Coffin Through the Window

HAMPSHIRE, in common with most English counties, is the home of many public houses and inns rejoicing in the name Red Lion. It has been suggested that one of the reasons for the popularity of this title dates back to the Jacobean period (1603-1625) when James I adopted a red lion as his symbol.

Be that as it may, on the main road between Havant and Petersfield at Horndean is the Red Lion, now a public house and at one time a thriving coaching stop serving the large southern ports. It was also the home of the ghost of an elderly lady.

The first recorded reports of the hauntings came from Bob and Lucy Blandford, who became landlords in the late 1930s and were to remain for some years. Lucy described how, after they had been resident for about six months, she was walking towards the kitchen when she saw a little old lady wearing a long black skirt and a shawl. She said, "It was just the way she was dressed that made me look twice. Her skirt was nipped in at the waist, similar to the sort of garment worn by stylish ladies at the turn of the century, but it was the New Year and many people were still attending fancy dress parties. The ladies' toilet was in

that vicinity and anyone wishing to use it would be required to leave the bar, walk along the corridor and past the kitchen. Therefore I was used to customers coming and going."

Very little more was thought about the incident until a few weeks later when her husband, Bob, saw a lady walking along the corridor as if unsure of her destination. He asked if he could help and pointed her politely in the direction of the ladies' toilet. Instead of looking round and acknowledging him, she walked straight into the kitchen and disappeared. It was only then that he realised the elderly lady was dressed in a similar skirt and shawl which Lucy had described a few weeks earlier.

Puzzled and more than a little scared, he decided to ask a few of the locals about the sightings and possible spectres in the pub. One gentleman who was a regular customer but not one who was prone to drinking more than his fair share, stated that at different times when he had been drinking at the bar he had felt a hand touch his arm as if someone wished to divert his attention, but when turning to respond there was never anyone in the vicinity. When questioned further, other locals said that for many years the inn had been haunted

The new staircase at the Red Lion, Horndean.

Remains of the spiral staircase at the Red Lion.

by a lady dressed in black and two or three of them swore they had seen the apparition near the stairway to the back cellar. They were a little reluctant to be more forthcoming as the Blandfords, as new landlords, were proving very popular and they did not wish to give the impression that things were amiss at the Red Lion. It had been some time since anyone had reported the old lady's appearance, but now it seemed, for no apparent reason, that the haunting had started again.

The Blandfords, in their turn, were sceptical of spectral existence in any form, although they were unable to deny that the lady had been seen by both of them, on one occasion after closing time. After discussion the couple decided to treat the idea of a ghost with humour and the proverbial pinch of salt and resigned themselves to accept the appearances of the ghostly lady.

That was until events became more serious. One day, some months later, Lucy was upstairs cleaning one of the bedrooms after a guest had left and was shaking a duster out of the window when she received a distinct push in the back, as if someone were trying to push her out. It was her husband who received the full tirade when she accused him of playing practical jokes. Many minutes and much angry conversation elapsed before he could convince her that he had nothing to do with the incident as at the time he was with a brewery representative in the cellar.

It was at this point that they both agreed that something would have to be done to find out a little more about the little old lady. Was she trying to tell them something and who was she anyway?

During the next week one of the barmen reported that the old fashioned latch which locked the back door opened on different occasions apparently by itself. When he opened the door – nothing! No one was there. He would immediately come back in, lock the door and before he reached the bar would hear the latch being lifted again. Although security locked when there were no guests, the windows in the bedroom where Lucy had received the push, would be mysteriously opened in the night by strange hands, strange because only Bob and Lucy were sleeping in the inn at the time.

It was only after much questioning and more research that the Blandfords learned that the description of the lady fitted that of a Mrs Byden, one time landlady of the Red Lion.

It appears that in the mid-19th century Mrs Byden died in bed after suffering a heart attack. Her body was found next morning by staff when they took up her morning beverage. Shocked by their discovery they immediately called the necessary authorities.

The usual formalities over, the undertakers put her in her coffin in order that the wake could take place. On the day of her funeral they found, to their horror, that the small, near spiral staircase would not accommodate the coffin with any dignity so they decided that the upstairs window be removed and the coffin containing Mrs Byden be lowered to street level and the waiting hearse – it was the same window through which Lucy was shaking the duster when she was pushed.

Soon after hearing this story, Bob was working near the beer cellar when the spectre of the lady came up the steps, passed through the cellar flap, turned left and walked towards the old wash house. After much discussion it seemed to everyone who had seen the ghost that she always appeared from the vicinity of this cellar.

The landlord then decided to put some new ideas into practice for the modernisation of the building. A new beer cellar was constructed and the old cellar was blocked. At the same time a new staircase was added. The wash house area was removed, as was the old spiral staircase leading from it to the corridor and kitchen, and the hauntings ceased.

The Blandfords left the inn many years ago. The present landlords, Mary and Mick McGee, who took over in 1992 assured me that they are unaware of anything unusual and have certainly experienced no hauntings, but there is sometimes a cold spot where they understand the old cellar stairs and wash room area once were.

Is the story of the coffin true? That old Mrs Byden died in that particular bedroom is an historically verified fact and it was certainly true that coffins were sometimes lowered through windows when it proved impossible to get them out any other way. Did this offend her dignity? Was the spectre that of Mrs Byden, and what was the significance of the cellar?

Siege of Old Basing

NOT far from Romsey, the pretty twin villages of East and West Wellow snuggle sleepily off the beaten track and, in common with many other of our Hampshire villages and hamlets, are quite content to allow the rest of the world to go by. Even so, East Wellow has seen action, especially during the time of Oliver Cromwell. It was from there that he planned the last stages of the Civil War in the south. It was at East Wellow that the legendary Cromwellian Colonel William Norton was to meet his untimely death and it is in the lonely lanes of East Wellow that the spectre of William Norton is often seen. One particular report was given to me by a resident of the village. He said that he had often seen Colonel William Norton in full regalia of battle walking between the manor house and the church.

Another sighting takes us north to the town of Old Basing and the small village of Oliver's Dell. It is here that Oliver Cromwell planned the raid which was to bring about the longest siege in the Civil War which lasted from May until

Old Basing showing the 17th and 18th-century cottage opposite the ruins of Basing House.

The present entrance to the ruins of Basing House.

November 1644, and again in 1665, from July until October when the final battle was led by Cromwell himself. The spectre often manifesting himself at Oliver's Dell is believed to be that of Cromwell, urging his men against the entrenched Cavaliers in the area.

From the long siege of Basing House, owned by the Lord High Treasurer, much fighting was to take place. It is said that Cromwell's Ironside army died in such numbers that at one time they afforded a barricade against the attacking troops. The village of Old Basing is still dominated by both the physical and atmospheric presence of Basing House,

now laying in ruins having been virtually destroyed during the siege. The site was subsequently turned into a garden, and during the 19th century a canal was cut through part of it. There have been many reports of ghostly soldiers walking as if lost or looking for friends and all the reports state that the spectres have a look of disbelief on their faces. One sighting in particular, which has been reported for over two centuries, is that of a Cavalier dressed with his full lace ruffles and long wavey hair. He is seen riding along the country lane (now the A30) carrying a broken sword. Although research does not show whether the

St Margaret's Church, East Wellow, burial place of Florence Nightingale.

above reports have any foundation in history, we do know that many good Englishmen on both sides were to lose their lives in the Civil War. Returning to East Wellow, another claim to the fame enjoyed by this village is that Florence Nightingale, although born in Florence, was the daughter of William Edward Nightingale of Embly Park, East Wellow. When a small child she returned to the family home in which she was brought up as a girl. In fact, all her life and even at the height of her fame, Embly Park was always regarded by her as home.

This great Lady With The Lamp, fam-ed for her bravery and nursing exploits, died in 1910 and was buried at East Wellow in the Church of St Margaret's where she was a regular worshipper.

Embly Park, now a school, is haunted, though strangely, not by Florence Nightingale, but by a coachman. No one knows just who he was, but he regularly takes his phantom coach and horses out of the drive of Embly Park and across the fields and meadows at great speed, disappearing just before he reaches the church. He is purported to be friendly, always smiling and even the children at the school look forward to his next visit.

The grave of Florence Nightingale in St Margaret's Churchyard.

Legend in East Wellow has it that anyone who visits the church, opens the door and notices St Christopher carrying a child, will be safe for the day.

The village of Wherwell situated in the beautiful Test Valley and about three miles south of Andover is historically regarded as the village in which was founded one of the most important convents in the country.

In the church of St Peter and the Holy Cross lies the sculpture of a nun who was once reputed to be the prioress of the convent. Now, alas only a ruined 17th-century wall remains as part of the devastation which occurred during Henry VIII's Dissolution of the Monasteries.

It is thought that a sleeping figure of the nun in the church may be that of Queen Elfreida, who founded the priory in the 10th century as a penance. Elfrieda was the Saxon Queen and wife of Edgar, first King of all England, but it is said that all her life she suffered from fits of guilt on two main counts. Edgar was her second husband, her first being Ethelwold by whom she had a son, Ethelred (The Unready). Edgar already had a son, her stepson Edward. It is said that she plotted in the murder of her first husband Ethelwold so that she could become Queen and on the death of Edgar, also plotted to have her stepson Edward murdered at Corfe Castle in the

Wherwell's thatched cottage opposite the Post Office and showing the war memorial.

year 978 in order that Ethelred could become king.

I would have thought it rather debatable that such an evil and grasping woman could suffer with 'pangs of conscience' but it is historically reported that Elfreida founded the nunnery at Wherwell and retired from the world in order to atone for her grievous sins and clothed her pampered body in hair cloth, slept at night upon the ground with no pillow and punished herself with every kind of penance. Many hauntings have been reported in this quiet village and nearly all of them are to do in some way with Elfreida and the nunnery. In the early 1900s the rector and his family would often see an austerely dressed figure of a nun walking around the churchyard. They kept quiet about it ,mainly because of their position, but one of their guests who witnessed the spectre could not be persuaded to remain as silent. After research the ghost was believed to be that of a nun who was bricked up alive in the nunnery wall as a punishment for some grave sin. Precisely just what ghastly crime the poor woman had committed was never revealed.

Such was the suspicion which surrounded the nunnery that peasants at the time were convinced that two evil

Wherwell Church of St Peter's and the Holy Cross.

looking monster heads, which were originally part of the corbel table in the church, were something to do with the story of a cockatrice – a serpent-like creature hatched from a chicken's egg and which had the wings of a duck and the tail of a dragon and was reared by the nuns of the authority of Elfreida within the confines of the priory. Any subsequent death in the village would be blamed on the creature who developed a liking for human flesh and would kill just by staring into the eyes of its victim. In the end it was cornered and killed itself by looking at its own reflection in glass.

It is also believed that even to this day, Elfreida and some of her followers are seen as nuns from time to time, carrying candles. They appear at dusk in the late autumn and frequent the churchyard and the ruins of the priory.

Does the wicked Queen still suffer with remorse, thus preventing her from eternal rest? Was she responsible in some way for the cruel punishment of the nun who walks the churchyard? How far is the legend of the cockatrice to do with the carved heads, which are now, incidentally, in the churchyard guarding the Victorian family tomb of

Mediaeval monster heads from the corbel table of the original Wherwell church and incorporated into the Victorian Iremonger family mausoleum, situated in the churchyard.

the Iremongers? It is for you and you alone to decide.

Crofton, Hampshire

CROFTON, just south of Titchfield, boasts a chapel of ease, thought to have been built by the monks of Titchfield Abbey, while the nearby Parish Church of the Holy Rood (noted in the Domesday Book) and the Crofton Manor Hotel, it has been suggested, were linked together by underground passages

From my own investigations, it is likely that the church and the hotel could have been linked, for at one time, monks used what is now the hotel as a dormitory. Not too long ago a guest at the Manor Hotel woke in the night to see a spectre of a monk sitting at the foot of his bed. Startled by the apparition and especially after having woken suddenly, he cried out in fear and the ghostly figure disappeared.

There have been many sightings of this ghostly monk wandering around the area of the church and manor. Mrs Humberdon and her son Peter, who lived in Oldham, Lancashire, were on holiday touring the south and had stopped to look at Crofton Church. Walking towards the altar she saw the ghost of a monk coming towards her. I asked how she knew it was a ghost and she replied: "At the time I was so transfixed with what I saw. He was in a robe which I can only describe as translucent. I suddenly realised that his face and his hands were the same colour as his robe. He took three or four steps towards me as if to say something, smiled and then disappeared. I turned to Peter, only to find that he was laying at my feet. As I bent down towards him, he opened his eyes and said, 'Mummy, the man said thank you.' Fearing for our sanity I left the church, returned to the hotel, collected our cases and returned home."

Many others, like Mrs Humberdon, have sworn that they have seen the spectre of a monk in Crofton.

Many residents and guests staying at the Manor Hotel have reported hearing footsteps and on occasions the violent sound of rattling barn doors coming from the courtyard. There have been reports of cigar smoke and the sweet smell of perfume both from the area of the church and the kitchens of the manor. The spectre of an old sailor and another of a beautiful lady have often been seen in the vicinity.

A few miles north of Crofton are the ruins of Titchfield Abbey, founded in 1222 by Sir Thomas Wriothesley, and it is around this area that for centuries, the manifestation of a monk has been seen. In recent years it has appeared in the back seat of motor vehicles using the A27.

It seems to be its sole purpose to frighten the drivers until they are about to lose control, then it disappears. The last sightings were in 1978 when two people were killed in automobile accidents on that stretch of road. Over this period there were many other documented accidents.

Is there any connection?

Northney, Hayling Island, Hampshire

HERE, the church is supposed to have the ghost of a sailor who walks the nave but there seems to be no first-hand experience of the haunting. Mr James Poor, one of the church officials, has never experienced any paranormal sighting and knows of no one who has actually seen the ghost.

This was an enquiry which we immediately aborted, but as is so often the case, it led to a much more authentic account of the haunting of a manor house.

I had the great pleasure to talk to Colonel L.E.Shepherd, who once owned the manor but by then lived in a lovely house on the seafront.

The colonel, an extremely down-to-earth retired officer, experienced a definite manifestation when he was living in Old Fleet Manor. The house was built in the 15th century and was reputed to be the oldest house on Hayling Island. The Shepherds bought it in 1943 and lived there until approximately 1960. Prior to that the house had been the property of a yeoman farmer (a smallholder who cultivates land). It is interesting to note that Old Fleet Manor had been built very near to a priory and may even have been part of it at one time, but had been put to use as accommodation for farm staff on the Dissolution of the Monasteries.

The history of the house is sketchy and very little in the way of documentation is available, but whatever happened there over the centuries, it seemed to be haunted by the apparition of a man in black. This spectre is well authenticated and has been seen quite a number of times by different guests and staff. Colonel Shepherd said that he often met the ghost in different parts of the house and at different times. "There were no regular visits – well, after all I suppose he lives there really. He just appeared and disappeared again." The spirit was friendly and posed no threat. "Even the family dogs and cats would stand aside as if waiting for him to pass," said the colonel. He related that on one occasion during an afternoon when he was resting on his favourite armchair in the lounge, a new puppy made a bee line for the open window and jumped out of it rather than remain in the room. Luckily the room was on the ground floor. "After that, the little fellow met the ghost several times, but seemed to make friends. he never ran away after that."

One of the spectre's favourite parts of the house was the spare bedroom on the first floor. Many times it would manifest itself especially when the domestic was working in there. It seemed that he was rather fond of that particular lady who apparently reciprocated his feelings and described the ghost as 'friendly and causing no distress or fear to anyone'.

There is one outstanding example of the haunting. On another occasion, again when the colonel was resting, he felt someone stroking his head, a phenomenon which had been reported as happening to other people when staying in the house and was not regarded as nasty or terrifying by any of them.

In 1960, Colonel Shepherd reluctantly sold the Manor to another retired military officer, Captain Illingworth. He met the spectre on a number of occasions and again experienced no unease but was quite happy to share the house with him. Apparently one of his new domestics also met the spectre, but for some reason was not quite so keen on renewing his acquaintance. She handed in her notice and left within the week.

Colonel Shepherd's explanation is that the ghost may have been that of a priest,

his black garb and the head stroking possibly an act of blessing. Maybe he had been connected in some way with the long defunct priory

This man in black may have enjoyed a priestly calling and may still consider that his work on this earth has not yet finished. Maybe he still wants to comfort people who are tired or sad. We do not know, but of this we are certain, many people have been able to confirm Colonel Shepherd's story.

Chilworth, Hampshire

IT IS in this old village that we stop and investigate some reported weird sounds which occur in and around a 17th-century cottage, part of a group of such cottages which are now in between a few modern bungalows peppered about the village.

Walnut Cottage, a timbered and white-walled dwelling, was bought originally as two cottages in about 1667 when Charles II paid many visits to the area. It was built then on the edge of the manor estate and housed estate workers.

During the last century it was reported that Walnut Cottage was haunted and no one wanted it. It was true that it was empty for some time during the 1850s. It had been a school but then it was sold and soon after became a small guest house. The first reports of hauntings were made by a group of lodgers who one night rushed out into the village seeking other accommodation, refusing to stay at Walnut Cottage for another minute.

There are other reports, some of which I consider a little hackneyed and none are brimming with credibility. However, reports have been published of hauntings in this century which are much more authentic.

In 1922, Mr and Mrs Withers from Glasgow were staying at the guest house when they suddenly woke one night to find that their eiderdown was glowing as if alight, but there was no heat from it.

In 1939, this phenomenon was repeated and this time the victim was the owner of the house, Mrs MacRea. Soon after that, Mr MacRea was sitting in the parlour when he saw, sitting opposite him and apparently warming himself by the fire, a pleasant looking man wearing a tasselled cap.

The spectre was accompanied by the sound of guttural voices coming from beneath the floor, but it was not loud enough to be clear.

The cellar had been long since filled in, but the MacReas called in a medium who definitely declared the place haunted.

Some visitors of the MacReas had children who were terrified one evening by the sound of a heavy and deep breathing animal making its way up the stairs in front of them and often the sound of a ghostly barking dog would be heard. Once, Mrs MacRea heard panes of glass breaking and the distinct sound of crockery being smashed but saw nothing. Mr MacRea would often be summoned to the front door when he heard a knock and would open it to find nothing.

Horses have been heard where there were none and the sound of furniture being dragged across the floor in rooms where there was no furniture.

The stairs, too, had their share of a significant amount of ghostly traffic

From the 1950s to the 1970s, a period of about 20 years, things quietened down to virtually nothing but then it all started again. There was the sound of people going upstairs, to the bathroom and washing their hands after running the water – yet none of the upstairs rooms have running water or wash basins.

I wonder if the medium was more forthcoming to the MacReas. They certainly never threw any light on the situation. It seems that the friends who stay in Walnut Cottage are not keen on identification. Well, maybe one day.

Buy Hopfields and Die

WHEN I first met Mrs Sheila White, whose husband had been a well respected GP in St Helen's on the Isle of Wight, I immediately felt comfortable and at ease in her presence. I was given a drink and ushered into a spacious armchair. I had arranged this visit to further research the weird and unanswered sightings they had on that January evening in 1969 when crossing Mersley Down as recorded in an earlier chapter.

After relating her experience of that incident, Sheila then asked if I would be interested in another story of the paranormal in which she was involved as a child.

"Something even more macabre than Mersley," she said, and quickly added, "But that maybe is because I was just a child at the time." Declining a further drink, I listened as Sheila White told me of a series of visits to Waterlooville all those years ago.

It concerned a house called Hopfields, which was built early in the 19th century when the area was composed largely of hopfields. The house has long since been turned into flats and is now part of the modern urbanisation of that area of Hampshire.

Edward Fawkes, a gentleman of comfortable means, liked the then rural aspect of the area and built Hopfields in order to spend his retirement years in the peaceful surroundings. Sheila White said, "I did not know very much about the man, or what he did, but he is believed to have held a directorship in the City of London."

His express wish after taking possession of Hopfields was that when he died, his descendants, of whom there were many, would pass the property down the line of future generations. That way Hopfields would remain in the Fawkes family for ever.

The phrase 'for ever' is all encompassing and the wishes of Edward were to hold good until the early 1900s, when it is recorded by Helen, great-granddaughter of Fawkes, that when she was ten, her father, who hated the house, found an excuse to move to Southsea where he had his business. At that stage he decided to keep Hopfields and let it furnished on a three-year renewable lease to a retired naval officer and his wife. They had no children, entertained quite a bit and were apparently ardent students of the occult and matters psychic.

All was well for a time and the new couple were enjoying their retirement. The size of the house allowed them to accommodate many visitors from paranormal societies, and the peaceful surroundings enhanced their studies. Then, one evening when there were no guests, their idyllic life style was shattered. The couple were sitting in their lounge when what they described as a sharp, cold wind blew out candles, buffeted the curtains and all but extinguished the flames of the log fire. Both sat there transfixed. In a diary (or log, as the naval officer described it) the ghost somehow managed to identify itself as Edward Fawkes and threatened violence unless they both moved from the house at once. They were given to understand that they had no right to be there and that there would be no peace for anyone but descendants of the Fawkes family and their staff. The officer sent a swift letter to Helen's father at Southsea, who at first took little notice, presuming its contents to be the fancies of an eccentric but harmless couple who were rapidly approaching senility anyway. However, events were to take on a different turn when a few weeks later another communique arrived. This second letter stated that it was quite impossible for both the retired officer and his wife to remain there because of the continuing manifestations and threats by Fawkes and they requested permission to sub-let for the remainder of their lease.

This was agreed and the property was sub-let to a middle-aged woman and her daughter who were both young enough to enjoy riding their horses in the countryside and joining in various local pursuits. After a while, Fawkes appeared again, this time threatening violence and even death to the two ladies.

Neither took much notice of the spectral appearances of Edward until, one year later, when the mother died in her sleep. At the subsequent inquest no medical condition for the cause of her death could be found. The coroner recorded a verdict of death by natural causes. The distraught daughter now gave credence to the hauntings which had so plagued her mother and herself and begged to be allowed to give up the rest of the sub-lease. Helen's father gave his consent and the girl quickly moved out. The family, now not only concerned but a little frightened, decided that Hopfields should be sold rather than them endeavouring to find another tenant. Eventually, it was bought by another service officer, this time a retired army captain. He had just returned from many years' service overseas and wished to buy a house in the Hampshire countryside in which he and his wife could spend their retirement years. Captain and Mrs Playfair soon redecorated the house and engaged staff. The walls of the captain's study were lined with many Indian artifacts including ornate daggers and swords. All seemed well until, about eight months later the body of Captain Playfair was found spreadeagled on the hall floor with one of his own jewel-bedecked Indian daggers embedded in his back. Mrs Playfair was in a totally incoherent state and was taken to stay with relatives. She made very little progress and was soon after transferred to a mental hospital where she eventually died without regaining her senses. Even though police and other experts worked on the case for many years, they could find no clues as to who had committed the murder. Was it connected to the threats from Edward Fawkes?

Once more the house was placed on the market and for a long time remained empty until it was eventually purchased by the wealthy Nowell family in the 1920s. The new owners very quickly set about transforming Hopfields from a gaunt sinister Victorian building to a modern and beautiful home. The connection with Sheila White and her family commenced at this point as they were great friends of the Nowells. Sheila, being of similar age to the Nowell children, was often asked to spend time with them at Hopfields during the school holidays.

Sheila said, "I never really liked Hopfields, but our family often visited. There was a feeling of evil about the place, especially one of the stairways, but it was not until a later visit that I experienced anything more."

One Christmas, after the Nowells had completely renovated and changed Hopfields, the Whites were asked to spend the festive season there together with their pet dog, Scraggy.

The first night, Sheila woke to the unusual sound of Scraggy growling, unusual because he was such a sweet natured little animal. She reached out to switch on the bedside lamp but the unfamiliar surroundings prevented her from finding it. She sat up and received a crack on the head, as if an iron bar had

struck her, so she dropped back and slowly sat up again – and the same thing happened

Scraggy was now growling much more frequently. It was then that Sheila started to feel panic, as if she were imprisoned in a sort of cage. But even at her tender age, she was able to collect her thoughts and came to the conclusion that somehow, during a restless night, she had managed to fall out of bed and end up underneath it. That probably caused her to hit her head on the springs every time she sat up.

She groped around and soon discovered that this was the case, so sliding out, found her way to the bedside lamp and switched it on. There in the corner, trembling in his basket, was Scraggy. His hackles had risen and he was still growling as he stared in the direction of the door.

He crouched in his basket, trembling with fear, his eyes transfixed. As Sheila looked at him, the handle of the door suddenly turned and the door opened, but no one was there. Sheila had had enough. Picking up Scraggy, basket and all, she ran terrified into her parents' room. The time was 1am.

For the rest of their Christmas stay in Hopfields, Sheila's father used that bedroom, but he also found that the door would suddenly open by itself and he became so fed up with closing it time after time, that eventually he just left it open. He reported no other paranormal experiences and the matter was not mentioned to their hosts. On subsequent visits, Sheila and her father would hear noises and see other things which scared them a little, but as only the two of them were involved, they decided not to make mention of these matters for fear of ridicule.

In retrospect perhaps it would have been better if Mr White or Sheila had told the Nowells about their experiences. If Captain Playfair had known about the 'curse' upon those occupying the premises who were not of the Fawkes line, would he have still purchased it? Could not Helen's father have been more forthcoming before selling the property? All too soon tragedy struck yet again. The Nowells had a son, a clever young man who was on vacation from Oxford. He was one of those young men with no apparent worries or troubles. He was just a carefree student who was promised a brilliant future. One morning he went down into the basement of Hopfields and, for no apparent reason, loaded a shotgun, placed it against his temple and discharged both barrels. His mother, so distraught with the needless and motive-less death of her son, soon died from a heart attack. Mr Nowell was so overcome by grief that he began to lead the life of a hermit, ignoring his daughter and refusing to see his friends. Shortly afterwards, he was also found dead in his bed. At the time, many commented that he died from a 'broken heart', but those who knew the house and its reputation were not convinced. The young Nowell girl was taken to a place of safety, never to return.

Due to the evil reputation the house had gained, it remained empty for many years and began to deteriorate so much that it was boarded up. Shunned by the locals in Waterlooville, it was sold twice more before being turned into flats amid the maze of dwellings which constitutes the modern town. No further reports of hauntings are obtainable, but one often wonders whether any of the occupants of the flats are subjected to manifestations, whether they even know the story, or whether the hauntings have naturally ceased now that Hopfields, as a single house, is no more.

The Killing of a Cook

ONE of the most impressive buildings in the area of Millbrook is Testwood House. Its original name was Little Testwood and its first owner, Sir Richard Dayrell, farmed vast estates. Sir Richard, one of the wealthiest farmers and country squires in 15th century Hampshire, often entertained on a lavish scale and received royal and society guests for weekend house parties. Even after his death, the house was often used as a lodge by Henry VII and Henry VIII when indulging in their hunting parties.

It is also said that Testwood House is one of the most haunted in the south, but this claim has been laid in respect of many other large country houses, so who can tell?

The first documented reports of a spectre date from the mid to late 18th century when one of the staff, described variously as 'the butler', 'the coachman' or 'the footman' was involved in a scandal. Research has since ascertained that by his style of dress and his mode of living the spectre was probably that of a coachman but we may never be privileged to know exactly his occupation as the only two reports in existence describe him as 'a senior member of the staff'. Let us therefore, for the sake of this well authenticated story, refer to him as 'the Coachman'.

This man, it seems, was enjoying an affair with the beautiful young lady cook. In large houses at the latter part of the 18th and beginning of the 19th centuries, cooks, by nature of their occupation and experience, were nearly always middle aged and slightly dumpy, but this young lady, it is said, was young, slim and beautiful in the extreme. What happened we do not know, but it was possible that someone in her position either did not choose, or found that it was extremely difficult, to keep faithful to the coachman, who one night discovered her in a compromising position with a junior member of the household and dismissed him immediately. Members of the staff heard raised voices and swore they were those of the cook and the coachman. Eventually, the argument ceased and it was presumed that they had both retired to their sleeping quarters, the girl to the attic and the coachman to his room over the stable. Imagine then the horror of an unsuspecting villager who the next morning found the body of the beautiful cook in the lane opposite the main entrance to Testwood House. When the villagers heard the story of the arguments between the coachman and the cook and after the subsequent discovery of her body, they renamed the small lane Cook's Lane and so it is known to this day. The murderer was never identified.

It was a visitor to Testwood House

who was to be the first witness to this gruesome ghostly sighting when he stood transfixed as two shady figures appeared, one apparently dragging the other. As they neared the spot where he stood, the air turned ice cold.

Unable to move, he watched them pass and by their costume he saw that it was a coachman dragging a young and beautiful girl. These spectres proceeded out through the gate and into the lane. It is reported that he said, "The figures came downstairs from the direction of the attic."

There are reports that for many years the sounds of galloping hooves and horse-drawn carriages were heard coming from the drive.

Ghostly sightings still occur inside the house and always seem to be associated with the coachman or with the murder. The attic room in which the young cook slept seems to be haunted, many scuffles and screams being heard in the middle of the night, but investigation, reveals nothing. The sound of loud footsteps on the floorboards in the attic is often heard, even though the area has long since been carpeted, and the sound of something being dragged comes from the stairs. Over the years, pet dogs and cats have avoided the area.

One day in the 1950s a lady guest reported seeing a maid, who by her dress and description matched that of the young cook. Said the guest, "I thought she was dressed in a rather strange way, but I was just about to ask her a question when she vanished by walking straight

through the wall. She had a sad look on her face." The guest was not frightened at all until the figure disappeared.

Outside in the courtyard, footsteps were often heard right up until about 1903, when for some inexplicable reason they suddenly ceased. It has now been reported, however, that from the late 1950s and early 1960s, the coachman began to make a nuisance of himself again. Once about that time, the care-taker's children were out playing when they saw him, dressed in a coachman's hat, buttoned coat and flowing robe.

Soon after this the property was taken over by Williams & Humbert Ltd and one of their chefs reported seeing the coachman. He said, "I have never seen anything closely resembling a ghost before or since, but this time there was no mistaking it. It was summer and I was standing in the kitchen preparing some onions and there was this man, dressed in a coachman's outfit, looking at me through the door of the kitchen. I asked him who he was and what he wanted and as I did so, he vanished into nothing. That's the only way I can describe it. I wasn't particularly frightened and I haven't seen him since."

Williams & Humbert were the fore-runners of the present owners who have asked that their names be withheld from this story. They told me that years ago, when it was still the property of Williams & Humbert, their company secretary was working late. He was annoyed to find that when he opened his door to leave (incidentally, the room in which he had been working was the murder attic), that all the lights had been turned off and he was compelled to grope his way down to the entrance.

He had vaguely heard some of the stories about the building and the hauntings but had taken no notice. He was a busy company secretary and had very little patience with fools, so cursing the cleaners and the caretaker for switching off the lights, he made his way down to the ground floor, only to see, seated at the reception desk in the hall and illuminated by the light which was coming from outside, the figure of a top-hatted man with his head tilted back as though enjoying a good laugh. He called twice, but the figure continued to laugh. It was then that he felt a cold and sinister atmosphere and realised that whatever the joke which was causing the figure to laugh, it was one which he had no inclination to share. He was chilled to the bone by this time, although the house was always well heated. The secretary rushed past the figure and out through the front door on to the drive, through the main gates and on into Cook's Lane.

On reflection he became annoyed at what he thought was someone who may have taken it into his head to play a practical joke. He was not the most popular of the bosses, often being described behind his back as an 'old woman' or a 'fuddy-duddy'. He determined that someone would be punished.

When notes were compared the next morning, the caretaker was adamant that he had left the lights on; in fact he had returned much later to switch them off. The village policeman whom he met in Cook's Lane went round with him as it was so late.

The coachman still seems to appear in many different places around the house and courtyard and he is doing many different things. He is always dressed in a long cloak-like coat, white trousers and some say he wears a fancy broad white waistcoat and that his cloak is tied with blue and white braid and it is said that his complexion varies from pale to pinkish.

Although his appearances are quite frequent, he always shows himself when a Wednesday falls on the 27th of the month, which we know was the date and day of the murder of the poor young cook.

Tradition also has it that the coach-man and his cook keep a rendezvous every December.

The Repulsive Sailor of Alverstoke

ALVERSTOKE is situated about a mile south-west of Gosport and is one of the most picturesque villages in the area. It still retains an old-fashioned air with its cobblestoned paths leading to the village shops, the church of St Mary, and the fine views from Stokes Bay over the Solent to the Isle of Wight.

It was here in the year 1812 that John Valentine Gray was born. The precise date remains uncertain, but his baptism at Gosport on 11 March 1812 is clearly documented. By the time he was six months old his mother had died and now lies buried in the local cemetery. It is believed that a few weeks later that his father was forced into the navy by the press gang, active in the area at that time. The boy was taken into Alverstoke workhouse (now a block of flats) and in October 1821 John Gray was apprenticed to Benjamin Davies, a chimney sweep living and working in Newport on the Isle Of Wight. No one then could have thought that this little lad, together with about three others, would change the course of history. John Gray was so maltreated by the sweep and his wife Margaret, that, three months after entering their service, he was found dead in the soot-laden basement cellar. At the sub-sequent trial which took place at Winchester Assizes under Sir James Burough, the indictment read: 'They, the Davies's, did this having not the fear of God before their eyes but being moved and seduced by the instigation of the Devil...'

After being found guilty of manslaughter, Margaret Davies was freed and her husband was fined one shilling. The people of Newport were so incensed with the treatment of the young sweep that they collected a penny subscription and raised a monument for him. The inscription reads, 'In testimony of the general feeling of suffering innocence.' The death of John Gray came to the notice of Ashley Cooper MP (later Lord Shaftesbury) who accelerated his efforts to steer a Bill through Parliament banning this sort of work for children. It took 53 years and more dead children before the Bill finally became law in 1875. Lord Shaftesbury noted in his diary, 'One hundred and two years have elapsed since the good Jonas Hanway brought the brutal iniquity before the public.' Hanway had, in fact, published revelations on the subject earlier in 1763 and again in 1765. He also published his recommendations for the formation of Friendly Societies for Master Sweeps.

Maybe it is a sobering thought that a

little innocent from Alverstoke who lived for a brief few months on the Isle of Wight, played such an important part in changing the country's social history. (See *A Brief Life* by Graham Bebbington)

To my knowledge, little John Gray has never been observed in spectral form, but his spirit still lives on, as does that of the champion of all ill-treated children, Lord Shaftesbury.

Reports through the centuries have, however, indicated that Alverstoke has not been completely lacking in sightings of the paranormal. Historians state that one of the most important buildings ever to be constructed here was Hasler Hospital which was completed in 1762 under the direction of the 4th Earl of Sandwich, John Montagu. It was he who gave his name to the sandwich as a snack to be eaten at the gaming tables. He was also a friend of Captain Cook who named the Sandwich Islands (now Hawaiian Islands) after him.

Sandwich was notoriously corrupt and was a member of Dashwood's Mad Monks of Medmenham Abbey or the Hell Fire Club, known and feared for their obscene and satanic cavortings in the Abbey ruins. Dashwood died in 1811 and John Montagu, Earl of Sandwich, 11 years later.

By then Hasler Hospital occupied an area of 33 acres and was built a mile or so from the coast in order to more easily accommodate the wounded from the Napoleonic Wars. It was well guarded but even so, patients and staff were thrown into panic when two figures

accurately described as those of Dashwood and Sandwich, wreaked havoc one September evening in 1812. Beds and furniture were overturned, obscene drawings materialised on walls and in offices. One doctor was attacked with a crowbar and another with a bayonet, both of which were thrown through the air.

Nothing more has been reported since, and that incident has never been explained, but was documented by many who were there and no doubt scared out of their wits at the time.

Another haunting involves a naval officer who, for reasons of security, asked that he should not be identified. He did indicate that for ease of narration I could use the name 'Nathan'.

As a boy, Nathan lived with his family and staff in a comfortable house in Alverstoke. He put his age at about ten when he experienced an occurrence which has remained with him to this day. The house, on the outskirts of this pretty village, had a large wall enclosing a formal garden with a neat lawn. At one time it had been a small cottage with Georgian casement type windows and its own stables.

Over the years the cottage had been enlarged somewhat but the windows with their small panes of glass had been retained. It was on one of these that a previous owner or visitor had scratched the name 'Mary Carboys'. Neither Nathan's family or the previous owners kept horses, but the stables were still used, now as coal cellars.

The family had been in the house for several years prior to anything unusual taking place. Nathan's father was away at sea, leaving his mother, sisters and the resident staff.

One evening, he complained to his mother that he was not feeling well and she accompanied him upstairs with the object of seeing him into bed. Being October and about 6pm it was a little dark and no lamps were lit anywhere in the house, so she left him on the middle landing, telling him to wait by the table in the passageway on which stood some candles while she went to fetch a lighted taper.

While he was waiting for her return, he was startled by the figure of a sailor, dressed in a blue jersey and wearing a stockinged cap who seemed to be scrutinising him with undue interest. The face of the spectre was repulsive, as if that of a sailor who was blind drunk, the sort that used to roam around on the hard at Portsmouth Dockyard.

He was just about to turn tail and run back downstairs when his mother appeared with the lighted taper and the sailor vanished.

Realising that something was wrong she asked Nathan what was the matter but dismissed his story as 'a lot of nonsense'. She did, however, search the whole house, but saw nothing unusual and heard no one.

The lad was so frightened, that for many weeks nothing would induce him to sleep on his own in the house.

Nathan's mother, a devout Christian, was sceptical of anything paranormal. But, knowing her son was not given to fantasy, she began to take the story seriously, thinking that he may have seen an old tramp who had broken in. Yet knowing she had made a thorough search of the house and found nothing, she was in a quandary as to what action she should take. After seeking advice from her church, she decided it would be best for Nathan if it were not mentioned again – as if nothing had taken place.

Six years later the family moved to Devon and the conversation turned to talk about domestic staff. Nathan had not forgotten the incident, although it was now very misty in his mind, but the talk about servants sparked off the question as to why, two years after the incident of the ghostly sailor, the cook and his nanny had left so suddenly. His mother told him that they, too, had seen the sailor on several occasions.

He asked her why she had said nothing then and was told that it was kept from him in order that he may be spared more distress as it may have affected his studies. He wanted to be a naval officer like his father and subsequently attained the rank of commander. Nathan's mother told him she had since heard that the house was reported to be haunted by the ghost of a sailor. There had been a murder there when it had been a small cottage. A young girl had been killed by a sailor. The cottage, standing as it did on the edge of a creek, had been a haunt of smugglers.

Prior to Nathan's family purchasing the

house, a previous owner was cleaning out the stables when one of the horses fell into a pit, the floor having given way under the animal's weight.Further examination revealed a smugglers' cellar with a passage leading out to the creek, but most intriguing was a small written account of the murder of a girl called Mary Carboys.

Who had left this old document? Was it a seaman? If so, was he the one seen in the house by Nathan?

Brief Spectral Sightings

WHEN I hear a report of a haunting or sighting, I endeavour to discover as much background information as possible, using various sources, such as old documents, and interviews with people concerned. However, to so many of them there is little or no explanation.

I intimated at the beginning of this book that a few of these may be the fermented imagination of some people, but others I treat much more seriously.

In this chapter I have listed just a few which I believe to be honest and forthright accounts of hauntings and sightings of spectres, but unfortunately, in respect of these particular experiences I have been unable to discover very much authentic background detail.

Aldershot

IN February 1675 an old woman, commonly called Old Mother Squalls could have changed the whole course of British history, for in the middle of the night she was summoned to the Fox and Hounds Inn, one of the oldest buildings in Aldershot. In secret she was called and secretly she attended.

Regarded by many as a witch, her activities left few doubting that she possessed supernatural powers. This night Old Mother Squalls, with the aid of a stick, made her way to the inn and learned that she was to deliver a child resulting from the union of King Charles II and Nell Gwynne. But despite all her power and knowledge, the child, a boy, was born dead. The parish priest was immediately summoned but was not happy to perform any rite or service, as the child had been conceived out of wedlock, born as illegitimate and died without the blessing of baptism.

The king, not willing to allow his son to be buried without the blessing of the church and in unconsecrated ground, bartered with the unyielding incumbent, finally settling a grant on the parish church of Aldershot for as long as the yew trees flourished there. The priest, satisfied with the bargain, placed the still-born babe in a small box and buried him under the yew trees in consecrated ground, just inside the churchyard.

This story of the birth of Nell's baby boy has been handed down through generations, although thorough searches of parish registers and church records show no mention of the incident ever

Holy Trinity Church, Aldershot.

having taken place. The ancient Fox and Hounds Inn was demolished long ago and on the site on which it was believed to have stood is now a charming house.

It is here and in the surrounding area that strange noises, similar to those of an old person shuffling along, accompanied by the tap, tap, tapping of a stick are heard and the indistinct apparition of a woman, bent almost double, is often seen. Over the centuries this ghost has been attributed to being that of Old Mother Squalls whom, it is said, lived in a hut nearby. Even to this day, dogs and cats refuse to go near and will turn tail and race away in the opposite direction.

There are also reports that those who have ventured out on dark February nights to visit the old yew trees in the cemetery have seen the apparition of a group of people in the vicinity of the churchyard gate, all of whom inexplicably disappear. Residents in a nearby house hear occasional dragging footsteps, always accompanied by the tolling of a bell.

Was Old Mother Squalls a witch and does she still walk the area? Maybe the footsteps accompanied by the bell are those of the incumbent who bartered

The village church of St Mary the Virgin, Bramshott.

away his principle and broke the Holy Orders of the day by interring an illegitimate babe in consecrated ground.

Bramshott and Buriton

TURNING from the main road running through Bramshott, we walk the short distance along a country lane which leads to the old manor. Little is known of the ghosts which haunt this lovely old house but there have been repeated sightings of a ghostly figure in white, thought to be that of Lady Hole, a former owner. Other sightings have been of two male ghosts, possibly Quakers.

Interior of St Mary the Virgin, Bramshott, showing the nave, the scene of the 'Grey Lady' sightings.

A short distance from the house and along another lane, ghostly music has been heard which some reports say originate from a shepherd boy. Nearby, in the same lane, the ghost of old Adam, a gamekeeper, sits to enjoy his evening clay pipe of tobacco.

The Bramshott parish church of St Mary the Virgin also boasts that it is the home of ghosts, for close by is the yew tree-bordered churchyard, where a little girl in a poke bonnet has often been seen walking through the rows of headstones. Other apparitions are the Bramshott Grey Lady and the ghost of a pot boy, still serving his pints to coach passengers. When talking to the villagers of Bramshott, I was told of a coach and horses, mounted Cavaliers clattering through the village, a horse carrying his murdered highwayman's body, a white animal which could possibly be a cat and even a black pig. Each person seemed to have his or her own pet ghost story to tell but many of these I took to be the fermentations of an over active imagination.

Travelling on through Petersfield we arrive at the village of Buriton and the picturesque Buriton Manor. It was here in the 18th century that Edward Gibbon was to write his classic work *The Rise and Fall of the Roman Empire*.

Much has been written about this manor, from the servant girl who committed suicide, underground passages and the proverbial brown-robed monks.

One thing, however, that stands out in the history of Buriton Manor is that in 1957 the owner, Lieut-Col Algernon Bonham-Carter, succeeded in having the rates reduced by £13 per year because the house was haunted. Facing the manor is a large tithe barn and tradition has it that a chambermaid hanged herself from its beams. She is often seen

The Manor House at Buriton.

Buriton – St Mary's Church.

passing through a solid wall, but it is well known that at one time there was a gate in the spot through which she passes. The underground passage used to be from the manor to Buriton Church and it is there that ghostly footsteps are often heard.

In 1962, the then owners, Mr and Mrs Miller-Sterling, reported that their five-year-old son complained that something or someone persistently tried to remove his pillow.

Some time ago, a son of one of the occupants was stabling his pony after an afternoon ride when he was startled to see a man standing next to the neatly stacked bales of hay. On moving closer to ask the visitor his business, he was surprised to see that the visitor was dressed in a long brown habit. Although there was really nothing to frighten him, he experienced a strong sensation of menace. As he stared, the figure simply faded. Too shocked to tell anyone about this solitary figure, he made an entry in his diary, detailing his encounter with the apparition. Some days later, his mother noticed the diary entry and called it to the attention of their priest.

The priest questioned the boy at some

The village pond at Buriton.

length and was shocked to find out that it appeared to be the same apparition which had manifested itself to his church warden and her daughter some months previously when they had been out gathering roses.

Part of the garden of the Old Rectory is known as The Monk's Walk and many have encountered the menacing figure of this friar wearing his brown cloak, tied at the waist with white cord. Why the spirit of the monk should appear we do not know. Why he can find no rest is a mystery that has never been answered.

Holybourne near Alton

LONG ago, when pilgrims travelled to Canterbury they would often stop at a small village by the side of the River Bourne and bathe in the pool which it was said possessed healing properties. So it is not hard to see how the name Holybourne came into being.

Today thankfully, the village seems to have been left behind in the race to turn our countryside into a vast tract of asphalt and concrete and, thanks to the

The Pool at Holybourne.

Holy Rood Church next to the pool at Holybourne.

hard work of local residents, Holy-bourne still remains a charming peaceful village with its pool preserved.

In this idyllic spot in the beautiful Hampshire countryside there stands a small cottage, the name of which was chosen by a ghost.

When it was purchased by the present owner, she had a visitation from a friendly ghost in the form of the manifestation of a grey lady. The ghost made it known that in life her name had been Anne. She had been resident in the cottage and had been very happy there.

146

Anne's Cottage, Holybourne.

The apparition then intimated that it would be happy if the name could be changed to that of Anne's Cottage, so the new owner, having as yet not chosen a name, duly complied with the ghost's request. Today, the owner and the ghost of Anne, the grey lady, live together in harmony at Anne's Cottage and the

spectre of Anne is often seen by the occupant.

Liphook, Hampshire

Liphook, similar to many towns in Hampshire, possessed an extremely old posting house called the Royal Anchor Inn which was located on the main coaching road to Portsmouth. In days gone by, many of noble birth had been entertained there and even Samuel Pepys was to note in his diary the enjoyable visit he paid to the Royal Anchor. Tradition accepts that Edward II visited in the year 1310. Many kings stayed there as well as other notables such as the Duke of Wellington and Lord Nelson. As with most royal resting places the Anchor Inn comes complete with a ghost, but this time, not that of royal blood but that of a commoner, a highwayman by the name of Captain Jacques.

Captain Jacques was attempting to ply his trade at Liphook when he was surprised by the appearance of Excise men. He fled to the An-

The Royal Anchor Inn at Liphook.

Displayed on the wall of the Royal Anchor Inn are framed details of the hauntings there.

chor Inn but after a chase was cornered in room number six. Knowing of a secret passage which opened up from behind the fireplace, he attempted to escape but was shot down.

From what we are able to glean about punishments meted out to 'footpads', his fate that day was better than if he had been captured, tried and found guilty. Since that day there have been many reports of sightings of Captain Jacques, not only in the hotel but also in the surrounding countryside.

The last reported sighting of him was by a lady visitor who occupied room six at the Royal Anchor. She had no prior knowledge of the room's reputation and over breakfast asked the landlord whether or not the inn was haunted. She spoke to him about a man, dressed in a long coat and tricorn hat who came out of the fireplace, walked across the room and through the closed door, not just once but three times in all.

On the third occasion the lady stated that she had opened the door and was in time to see the mysterious figure vanish on reaching the end of the passage, but

The fireplace at the Royal Anchor Inn, where Capt Jacques was shot.

explained that at no point was she frightened, being a person who had no fear of the supernatural. She had, in fact, returned to her bed and for the rest of the night enjoyed a sound sleep.

During my investigations in and around Liphook I also came upon many stories about a boy and his flute who had haunted the area for many centuries. I received many accounts of this boy walking beside a horse and gently playing his flute. On questioning people, there seemed to be doubt as to which spectral plain this apparition belongs. There appeared to be mixed feelings, some saying that he is a spirit and an equal number declaring that he is a fairy. My own personal opinion is the latter with the added word 'story', but then maybe I am doing a great injustice to those who suggest otherwise.

Newbridge, Isle of Wight

NEAR the southern coast of the Isle of Wight, just east of the village of Newbridge, is Dodpits Cross.

For those travellers who should chance to venture that way, however, no cross will be seen for it is just a junction with a signpost leaning slightly as if a heavy weight had been hung from its extremities.

One evening in October 1928, a young girl was making her way home from Shalfleet village school where she had stayed late for extra tuition for a forthcoming exam. Being a country girl she had no fear of the dark lanes, but as she neared the signpost, she experienced a feeling that all was not well. In the twilight even the signpost looked different. By now, being slightly fearful, she approached it, her fear turning to horror as she realised it was no longer a signpost but a gibbet, and hanging from its arm was the body of a man.

She could distinctly see his head held tightly in the noose, the rope parting his long shoulder-length curly hair. He was bearded and wearing a dark cloak. As his sightless eyes met hers, she snapped out of her state of mesmeric horror. Turning to flee to the safety of her home and her waiting parents, she was suddenly stopped, as if by unseen hands and turned once again to face the gibbet and its grisly burden. But, it had completely disappeared and the signpost had once more returned

During the course of many years she has been questioned about this incident but never once has her story changed, for so horrific was the scene that it has been etched on her mind and there would remain for the rest of her life

It is little wonder that Dodpits means 'The Pits of Death' and it is reputed that a highwayman was hanged at that spot

Dodpits Cross, Newbridge, Isle of Wight.

Odiham

It was from the village of Odiham in the year 1203, that King John set out for the historic meeting at Runnymede and to Odiham he was to return.

Odiham Castle, today a crumbling ruin, has been home to many kings over the years and also to Elizabeth I. But it is not with ghosts of kings, queens and other royal personages that the castle is haunted, but by that of a lowly minstrel. On clear moonlit evenings, especially in the autumn, are often heard the sweet notes of his flute and with them sometimes appears the spectre of the mins-

in the days of yesteryear. Could this be the reason why the bridle path leading from this haunted spot has been called Dark Lane from time immemorial?

Roman walls of the castle at Porchester.

Porchester – the Norman castle in the north-west corner of the Roman fort.

trel, often described as 'a thing of shreds and patches.' On the banks of the canal which links the old castle with the village of Greywell there have been many sightings of prisoners being escorted to and from the castle dungeons, their clothing that of yesteryear.

Many other reports have been received from people not actually seeing anything, but experiencing a feeling of impending doom, or an atmosphere of dread. One wonders just what caused such an atmosphere and the apparitions seen on this spot.

Porchester Castle

Not too many miles away , situated on

the northern boundary of Portsmouth Harbour, is Porchester Castle, again a castle which has enjoyed many royal connections. To name but a few, King John, Richard II, Henry I, Edward II, Edward III, all had a hand in the construction of different parts of the building. It is also said that Pontius Pilate, just prior to his death and troubled by conscience, sought solace in Porchester Castle, having travelled there by Roman galley.

Now, nothing more than an empty shell, this nine-acre site, first built on and inhabited by the Romans, stands as a constant reminder of the history that lies within.

No castle would be complete without its ghost, but in this case not a ghost of a particular person or groups of persons, but of a 'whitish' object which appears suddenly in dark corners. Two extremely practical businessmen reported seeing it independently but on the same day, at intervals of a few hours. Many other people who have witnessed it, describe it as a 'sort of shape'. It has been suggested that the apparition could be that of the ghost of an uninvited actor from the days when public performances of plays took place in the castle grounds, but the more plausible explanation which has been put forward by the majority is that the ghost was once a prisoner held in the dungeons of the castle and probably executed in the grounds. Will anyone ever be certain?

Haunted Pubs and Bars

MUCH history about the appearance of apparitions seems to centre on our hostelries, possibly because they were the central meeting places for much of the local population of villages and towns.

Today, with the much wider variety of entertainment, they have ceased to be the centre of attraction and I have endeavoured in this chapter to give mention to some of the more notable sightings of which no satisfactory explanation is forthcoming.

Many of these stories have an intriguing link to legend, such as the bloody murder in the Brushmaker's Arms at Upton.

Here we turn to a legend which is now some 400 years old. This is the story of a miserly brushmaker by the name of Chickett, who lived in a room above the bar. One night, thieves attacked him in his room, stole his money and left him to bleed to death. It has been reported that since then his plodding footsteps and the clink of coins, as if he is still sitting there counting his money, are heard and, for no apparent reason, doors rattle, dogs bristle and snarl at an unseen presence.

Another inn worth mentioning is the Hyde Tavern in Hyde Street, reputed to be the oldest tavern in the city of Winchester. Here it seems, many centuries ago, a poor woman begged lodgings for the night at the tavern, or if not, at least a warm by the fire. She was refused both with the words: "No money – no room!" Next morning the old woman was found at the rear of the tavern kitchen garden frozen solid. From that time the apparition was to be seen wandering in the vicinity of the tavern. There is also talk of a poltergeist haunting the Hyde. It has startled

The Hyde Tavern, Winchester.

Interior of the bar at the Hyde Tavern with landlady Valerie Dove.

serving girl working at the Swan was often seen to be too friendly with those she served. Her husband, a sailor, unexpectedly returned home and, enraged by her flirtation and in a jealous temper, murdered her.

From that day her ghostly form has from time to time been seen near the fireplace where she met her grisly end. Her apparition was reported as recently as 1991.

Travelling further south we come to the quiet and peaceful Langstone Harbour. Situated there is the Royal Oak, a centuries-old pub. It has often been said that a strange presence has been sensed and footsteps have sounded on empty

residents and guests alike by pulling the blankets slowly from the beds. Many would be woken in the middle of the night by the extreme cold, only to find the bedclothes in an untidy heap on the floor.

Another tragic tale concerns the White Swan in Portsmouth's Guildhall Walk. It happened during the late 1880s when a

The White Swan, Guildhall Walk, Portsmouth.

The tide and windmills at Langstone Harbour.

The Royal Oak at Langstone.

stairs and in corridors. People have been startled to hear the sound of chairs being scraped across the stone floor when there has been no one there. At one time, a businessman booked in to the Royal Oak for a three-day stay, but after only one night could not check out quickly enough, saying that something unseen had prowled around his room in the middle of the night.

However, I know of only one report of the ghost actually appearing. Mrs Joan Spring who lived there with her husband, the licensee, for 30 years, awoke one night to find a figure dressed in a white gown standing by the side of her bed. Thinking that it was her daughter Penny, who was prone to sleepwalking, she started to get out of bed. The figure in white turned, drifted silently across the room and vanished through the wall.

We must now return once again to the Isle of Wight and the village of Wootton. It was here that I was to meet David Death, a well-known Island motorcycle dealer.

He was to relate the tale of a large house, situated on the sea shore which had been turned into a licensed club. A single door led into this newly-constructed bar behind which David's daughter was standing. Suddenly it opened and David saw a lady who was wearing a well-cut grey two-piece suit, enter and walk to the other side of the room. His daughter crossed to get her order, only to find that the room was empty. Both she and David searched the premises, but there was no sign of her presence.

Who she was or why she should haunt that room we have no knowledge. Today, the club is closed and the old house has taken on an entirely different role.

I could not end this book without reporting a traditional tale, which I do with 'tongue in cheek'. It is a story which has been told many times since the early 19th century, of a wicked little fellow who was found in the tower of St Helen's Old Church by some masons from Portsmouth. They mocked him and for revenge he told them they would drown on the way home, which they did.

After his death he would often be seen in his long black coat, boarding the Bembridge to St Helen's ferry without paying his fare and always disappeared halfway across into a watery grave. A little tale that seems to have lost nothing over the last 200 years.

There is one thing of which I am certain above all others. Whatsoever we may think we know, whatsoever we may be told by other people, wheresoever we may go or whatsoever we may do, we do it under a WEB OF FEAR.